THE
IMITATION
OF
CHRIST

by
Thomas à Kempis

translated by
John Rooney

Published by:
Templegate Publishers
P.O. Box 5152
Springfield, IL
62705

ISBN: 0-87243-097-9

Manufactured in the United States of America

TABLE OF CONTENTS

BOOK ONE *Useful Hints on the Spiritual Life*

BOOK TWO   *The Life that is Inward*

BOOK THREE   *Inward Comfort*

BOOK FOUR   *The Sacrament of the Altar*
(A Devout Exhortation concerning Holy Communion)

Scripture quotations are taken, with permission, from The Jerusalem Bible © 1966 Darton, Longman and Todd and Doubleday and Company Inc.

This new English translation of 'De Imitatione Christi' can be regarded as a commemoration of the sixth centenary of the birth of its reputed author. Thomas à Kempis was born at Kempen in either 1379 or 1380 A.D. His father seems to have been a metal worker of some sort. Hence the family name, Hamerkin. His mother taught at the little village school. It is probable that she was Thomas' first teacher.

The great influence on his early education was, however, the successor of Gerard Groote, Florentius Radewijns, sometimes called Florentius of Deventer. Gerard Groote, founder of the Brothers of the Common Life, was an initiator of the strong religious movement known as the *Devotio Moderna*. Every bit as powerful as was the Oxford Movement in the nineteenth century, the influence of the *Devotio Moderna* continues today, largely on account of the popularity of Thomas à Kempis' book. The *Imitation* is generally regarded as the most complete and comprehensive statement of the principles of the *Devotio Moderna*.

Thomas à Kempis was very much attracted to the Brothers of the Common Life. He may have wished to join them. Yet in 1399 he joined a new Augustinian community at Mt St Agnes in Zwolle. It was three years, however, before he was accepted as a novice. Some have sought to explain this by suggesting that Thomas was a dullard or, more charitably, that life in the new monastery was somewhat chaotic at first. The most acceptable explanation seems to be that the three years were a period of hesitation during which Thomas and the community resolved doubts concerning the suitability of his committing himself to a monastery which had as its prior his own brother, John Hamerkin.

Ordained priest in 1413, Thomas lived a quiet life of study and meditation. He wrote several other devotional books besides the *Imitation*. His life's work centred, however, round the copying of the books of others. He was appointed sub-prior of the monastery for two short periods, but seems to have made quite a mess of the job on both occasions. For a time he was novice master, a task that was more congenial. He died at Mt St Agnes in 1471.

In 1672 Maximilian Hendrik, Prince-Bishop of Cologne, ordered Thomas' body to be exhumed and placed in a great reliquary. There was much talk of having Thomas canonized. Yet the process of beatification was never actually started. There is a legend that, when the body was exhumed, the inside of the coffin lid was severely scratched, suggesting that Thomas had been buried alive. The canonization process was then discontinued on the assumption that, in such circumstances, a man might easily despair. Thus far the legend. Scully, in his *Life of the Venerable Thomas à Kempis*, 1901, describes the exhumation in frankly adulatory terms, quoting Arnold Waeyer as his source. Scully does not mention the scratches. He points out that the death of Princess Isabelle of Belgium, the main lay promotor of the cause, prevented her doing anything to help the process. Maximilian Hendrik, the clerical promotor, became so involved in political troubles and upheavals that he was unable to find time to push the work ahead. In the late eighteenth century, Eusebius Amort declared his intention of promoting Thomas à Kempis' cause for beatification, but he never actually did anything about it.

After the Bible the *Imitation* has enjoyed more popularity than any other christian work. How do we explain this popularity?

Although it was written for the benefit of a monastic community, it has proved to be of great value to those who seek sanctity in the active life. It was written in an age when there was a great growth of personal piety among the faithful. Ordinary men and women, mothers and fathers of families, sought lives of greater perfection. In the *Imitation* they found an answer to their needs. Thomas à Kempis' work happened to be the right book at the right time.

Its continued popularity owes much to its simplicity and orthodoxy. By simplicity is not meant any quality of simple-mindedness. Its teaching has a homespun quality which is very telling. Also notable is its lack of doctrinaire positions or faddishness. True, now and again, the writer's pet dislikes, pilgrimages for example, come in for caustic mention. But even in this there is a certain restraint.

It may seem strange that orthodoxy should be mentioned in connection with the *Imitation*. For the mysticism of the middle ages has been interpreted as a reaction against the barren intellectualism of scholasticism. We can understand much of what the *Imitation* says about learning only in the light of this counter-reaction. Three main lines of mystical opposition to the schools can be discerned. The first, chronologically speaking, is the emotional approach represented by Hugo and Adam of St Victor. The second is the speculative school of German mystics represented by the Brothers of the Free Spirit and writers such as Meister Eckhart and Tauler. The third is a blend of these two and is the tradition of the *Imitation*. It owes much to the St Victors, via the writings of St Bernard of Clairvaux, and equally it draws from the German school through the teachings of Florentius of Deventer and of Ruysbroek. The orthodoxy of the *Imitation* is seen in that it keeps its feet always on the ground of doctrine and avoids the eccentricities that sometimes plagued the other schools.

I started to translate the *Imitation* with no thought for possible publication, but from a simple desire to understand what the book is all about. Most English translations of the past lack bite for the modern reader. Terms such as 'compunction' or 'mortification' have ceased to mean anything to the large majority of modern readers; and, where they mean anything at all, they have connotations quite beyond what was intended by the fifteenth century spiritual writer. The archaic terminology of the older translations, which is perhaps only half understood, gives the impression that the *Imitation* is more morbid, dreary and unsympathetic than it actually is.

There is no denying that the book has a starkness that gives many the creeps. This quality is just as much a product of the age in which the book was written as our revulsion is a product of the age in which we live. Thomas à Kempis' age was extremely concerned with guilt. Other ages have been tantalized by the meaning of life. Our age seems to be mesmerized by the purpose of life. This guilt consciousness of à Kempis' age demanded a special type of courage. The harsh realities of life in the later middle ages were no laughing matter. The philosophy that seemed best suited to answer the problems of a harsh guilt-ridden society seemed to be that of the stoics. The stoic virtue that was especially admired was 'Gravitas'. A man must always be in complete control of himself. Just as strong uncontrolled hate was abhorred, so also was undisciplined love and emotion. To gain the respect of his peers a wise man must be grave, apparently indifferent to trouble. Public laughter was frowned upon. Funnily enough, public tears were not. Awareness of influences such as these should help us to get to the core of à Kempis' message, free of the irritation that some of the starker passages arouse in us.

The original latin of the *Imitation* is not very polished. Ideally, a proper English translation should reflect its lack of polish. My translation avoids technical rigour. It is a rendering of a work which I hold in very high esteem. It endeavours to reproduce the thought of the *Imitation* as accurately as possible; but, where the meaning is a little obscure, this English translation is adapted to my own particular understanding. Whether I have done the author a service in this matter will be for others to judge. This is the reason why I have rendered expressions such as 'compunctio cordis' in some places as 'heartfelt sorrow', in others as 'remorse' or simply 'sorrow'. It is also the reason why groups of adjectives or adverbs are sometimes rendered by one composite phrase.

A criterion I have used in searching the more obscure meanings is to imagine how a Dutchman would have thought the sentence. The obvious example is of course the expression 'exterius scire'. Exterius scire = van buiten kennen = to know by heart. It has, however, further applications. The most important of these has been the translation of the latin conditional clauses. The latin word 'si' goes into Dutch as 'als'; but 'als' does not only mean 'if'. It also means 'when' and 'whenever'. I have felt justified, therefore, in rendering many conditional clauses as temporal clauses in English.

One of the qualities of the *Imitation* which I have tried to retain is its proverbial style. The book has always struck me as a set of notes, ready for expansion and explanation by a preacher. Continuity of development is sometimes lacking. I have tried to preserve this by making sentences as short as possible, sometimes breaking down the longer latin sentences into shorter ones and leaving out the connectors that English finds superfluous. Translation purists may be, and pedants certainly will be, horrified that I sometimes alter the order of the latin clauses. This is to restore the thought balance which is often lost through breaking the longer sentence down.

My approach in this is justified by the tradition that the *Imitation* arises out of a set of *ripiaria*. Gerard Groote and Florentius of Deventer encouraged the Brothers of the Common Life to make collections of sentences from the scriptures, from the fathers of the church and indeed from the classics. These collections were known as *ripiaria*, what I am fond of describing as 'festoons'. It is generally believed that the *Imitation* arose from Thomas à Kempis' reflections on such *ripiaria*. Some of his quotations are a little inaccurate. This can be explained by his paraphrasing for the sake of continuity.

The one area where I have been consciously and

deliberately inaccurate is in the translation of terms such as *devoti*. The term *devoti* was used to designate the followers of the *Devotio Moderna*. It has no exact modern English equivalent. I have chosen to translate the word as 'committed', sometimes simply as 'devoted' or 'devout'.

In view of the above, I present this translation in a spirit of diffidence. Anyone who wishes to share my understanding of the *Imitation* is welcome to do so. Friends have suggested to me that I should dedicate this work to the memory of the late Pope John Paul I, who loved the *Imitation*. Yet it would be presumptuous surely to dedicate this work to him. Instead I dedicate this book to all who read it. Let me ask those who find benefit in it to answer Thomas à Kempis' prayer:

> *When they receive the joy they yearned for, when they have enjoyed union with you, when they leave the sacred heavenly table, filled with comfort, please let them remember me, a sinner.*
>
> (Book 4, Chapter 17)

John Rooney
Mill Hill
LONDON

BOOK ONE

USEFUL HINTS ON THE SPIRITUAL LIFE

CHAPTER ONE

How to Follow Christ and be Detached from the Emptiness of the World

The Lord states: *He who follows me does not walk in darkness* (Jn 8: 12). These, Christ's words, advise us that if we wish to be really enlightened and to be freed from spiritual blindness, we must imitate the life style of Christ. Our deepest desire should be to reflect on Christ's life.

What Christ teaches is superior to all the teachings of the saints, and he who shares the spirit of Christ finds in his teaching a secret food. It happens, however, that many, although hearing the Gospel quite regularly, remain but little affected by it. They lack the spirit of Christ. If a man wishes to get the best out of the words of Christ, he ought to strive to model his whole life on Christ's life.

There is not much point in discussing the Trinity with the sort of conceit that is offensive to the Trinity. Indeed a man is not holy or divine because he speaks divinely. It is the holiness of his life that makes him dear to God. I had rather feel sorrow than know how to describe it. Knowing the bible by heart and familiarity with all the sayings of the philosophers are quite barren accomplishments in such as lack God's love and grace. Apart from the love and service of God *Vanity of Vanities. All is Vanity* (Eccl 1: 2). It is, therefore, the most wise course to become detached from the world and strive towards the kingdom of heaven.

It is worthless to pin your hopes on the search for perishable wealth, to yearn after status and position. It is pointless to submit to pleasure-centred wants and to strive after that for which you must later be punished. It is foolish to want a long life and pay little attention to the goodness of that life. It is daft to concern yourself with the present only and have no care for the future. It is madness to grasp at the quickly passing pleasures of the moment and be slow to go where joy is stable and lasting.

Remember the proverb: *Sight does not tire the eye nor hearing weary the ear.* (Ecc 1: 8). Strive, therefore, to withdraw your heart from concern for visible things and transfer your attention to the invisible. For such as follow the delights of the senses stain their conscience and lose God's grace.

CHAPTER TWO

How to Know Ourselves Humbly

Knowledge, despite man's natural desire for it, is worthless unless it is linked with the fear of God. By far the better course is that of the simple farmer who serves God than that of the proud philosopher who, neglectful of self, surveys the heavens. A man who knows himself values himself lightly and is little affected by human praise. If I lack charity, even the widest knowledge of human affairs is of little value to me before God. He will judge me by what I have done.

Control any excessive desire for knowledge; you will find it a great distraction and very deceiving. The knowledgeable like to be recognised and spoken of as wise. Much of what may be known is of little value to the soul. To search for anything other than what serves our salvation is indeed very unwise. The spirit is not satisfied by quantity of words; indeed the mind is refreshed by the goodness of one's life. Great trust in God is built upon a clear conscience.

If you have not lived well, you will be judged all the more harshly if you have been more fully and better informed. Do not, therefore, boast your skill or knowledge, but rather be fearful of the knowledge given to you. If you think that you know a lot and have quite superior intelligence, know also that there is much more that you do not know. *You have no reason for pride* (Rom 11: 20); but you should admit your ignorance all the more. Why should you want to be outstanding when there are so many others more learned and skilled in the law? If you want to know and learn something worthwhile, seek to be unknown and ignored.

A true knowledge and evaluation of self is the best and most worthwhile sort of learning. Perfect wisdom is having no great opinion of self and a good and high regard for others. Even if you see another sin openly or perform some serious deed, you should not, therefore, think the more highly of yourself. You do not know how long you can stay good. We are all weak. You should always regard yourself as the weakest.

CHAPTER THREE

Sound Teaching

It would be good if Truth himself taught us directly and not by means of words and images. Often our viewpoint and our understanding deceive us and we see but little. What is the point of heated discussion concerning obscure and abstruse matters such as our ignorance prevents our assessing? It is great stupidity indeed that neglects the worthwhile and necessary in favour of the curious and dangerous; we have eyes, but do not see.

Why should we bother about classifications and sub-classifications? He to whom the eternal word speaks is rescued from a multitude of opinions. From one word come all things and all speak one: that is *What I have told you from the outset* (Jn 8: 25). Without him there is neither proper understanding nor discernment. He in whom all things are one, who draws all into one and perceives all as one can keep us in constant peace of heart. O God of Truth, bind me to you in everlasting love! I am tired of reading and hearing so much; in you is all I wish and desire. Let all teachers hold their tongues, all creation be silent before you, but you alone speak to me.

The more at one with himself a man is, the more inwardly detached he is, so much the wider and the greater is his effortless understanding; for he is receptive to some light of understanding from above. His spirit, pure in its stout simplicity, is not weakened by many activities. It does all for God's honour and shines out as it is, careless of personal achievement. You will find that you have no greater hindrance and annoyance than your own uncontrolled desires. Before he does any outward deed, the good devout man considers carefully his motivation. These outward deeds do not attract him to lusts of any vicious tendency, but are subjected to his balanced judgement. Striving to control oneself is outstandingly difficult. This should be our task – to control self, daily to become more strong and always to reach towards improvement.

In this life all perfection is mixed with some imperfection. All our insight has some darkness. Humble self-knowledge is a surer way to God than deep scientific research. Knowledge itself is not to blame, nor any simple awareness of things well considered in the light of God's plan; but the better choice is to strive after a good conscience and a virtuous life. Many people err and achieve little good through excessive desire to know well and too little desire to live well.

If we expended as much effort in rooting out faults and instilling virtue as we do in arguing problems, then there would not be so many evil scandals to the people nor such great laxity in monasteries. When the day of judgement comes we will be asked not what books we read, but what deeds we did, not how well we spoke, but how religiously we lived. Tell me now what has become of those doctors and scholars, so renowned for learning while they lived. Others hold their positions now and I doubt that they are ever recalled to mind. Alive they were renowned, now nobody mentions them.

How speedily the good opinion of the world changes! Did they achieve any balance between their living and their learning? If they did, they were really

studious and very learned. For many fall because they
hunger for useless worldly knowledge and care little
for serving God. By the very fact that they choose
greatness rather than modesty, they lose all balanced
sense of personal value. To be great you must have
great love. To be great you must be small and place
little value on earthly recognition. To be prudent you
must judge earthly things as rubbish and strive to gain
Christ. To be learned you must submit to God's will
and give up your own will.

CHAPTER FOUR

Prudent Deeds

Do not trust in every word or emotion. Ponder each
matter with careful patience as God would. What a
pity that we are so weak that it is often the evil rather
than the good that we think or say of one another!
Properly balanced people do not believe every tale
they hear; for they understand man's weakness, his
tendency to evil and his easy surrender to talk.

It is certainly wise to avoid precipitate actions and
stubborn tenacity in one's personal views. To do this
means one should not too easily trust gossip nor rush
to spread the gossip we hear or believe. Take the advice
of a wise and prudent person and seek fuller infor-
mation rather than trust your own impressions. A
good life makes a man wise in God's eyes and makes
him learn much from experience. The humbler he is
and the more he bows before God, the more pleasing
and wise he will be.

CHAPTER FIVE

The Lesson of the Scriptures

In the scriptures we search for truth, not fair phrases.
It is fitting that scripture be read in that same spirit
in which it was written. Our search of scripture should
be directed more at usefulness than at the apt phrase.

We should be happy to read simple devout works
as well as the deeply profound. Do not let the author's
standing, whether he is of little or great learning,
affect your judgement. Let the love of pure truth
prompt you to read. You ought not to ask: Who said
this? Listen to what is said.

Men change, but *The Lord's faithfulness is eternal*
(Ps 117: 2). God speaks to us in different ways, but
without favouritism. Our own curiosity is often an
obstacle to our understanding of scripture in so far as
it tempts us to dally over argument and discussion
instead of simply reading on. To gain benefit, read
with pure humble fidelity and without any desire to
make a learned impression. Be free with your ques-
tions, pay respectful heed to the words of the saints
and be patient with old men's parables; they are not
uttered without purpose.

CHAPTER SIX

Undisciplined Desires

A man who wants something too badly suffers imme-
diate anxiety. The proud greedy man is never at rest;

but the poor meek man enjoys peace. A man who is not perfectly detached is easily tempted and is overcome even in the smallest and most trifling matters. Weak-spirited, carnal, influenced by emotion, he has great difficulty in disciplining his earthly wants; self-denial causes him great distress and he is easily irritated by the slightest opposition.

When he has given in to temptation, his conscience is racked with feelings of guilt; for his surrender to emotions helps him very little in his search for peace. It is by resisting emotions, not by surrender to them, that true peace of soul is found. Peace is to be found neither in the lustful nor in the worldly man, but in the warmly spiritual person.

CHAPTER SEVEN

Flight from Foolish Hope

It is foolish to build your hopes on men or created things. Do not be afraid to serve other men for the sake of Christ's love and to appear to be of little importance by the world's measure. Do not try to be self-sufficient. Place your trust in God. Do what you can. God will go along with your good intentions. Do not trust in what you know yourself, or in the skill of anyone else. Just trust in God's grace. God helps the meek and levels the proud.

Do not rejoice in the wealth that you have or in your influential friends, but give glory to God. He holds everything in being and seeks above all to give himself to you. Do not boast of your handsomely impressive physique. It takes so little to sicken and weaken it. Do not preen yourself on your facility of wit. You might offend God. It was he who gave you all your natural talents.

Do not regard yourself as better than others. In the eyes of God, who knows what is inside a man, you may be judged to be worse. Avoid conceit concerning your good deeds; for God's judgement varies from that of men and he is sometimes displeased by what men find attractive. If you have anything good, be sure that another has something better. This will keep you modest. You can come to no harm if you subject yourself to all; you can come to real harm if you place yourself above anybody. Lasting peace is with the meek; the heart of the proud man is full of greed and irritation.

CHAPTER EIGHT

Fear of Familiarity

Do not open your heart to every man (Eccl 8: 22). Bring your problem to a wise God-fearing person. Seek rarely the company of the young or of outsiders. Do not flatter the rich. Do not be seen willingly in the company of the powerful. Keep company with the meek, the simple and the devoutly virtuous to discuss uplifting topics.

Avoid familiarity with any one woman and commend all good women to God. Choose to be familiar only with God and his angels. Avoid the limelight.

You must be kind to all, but avoid familiarity. It

happens sometimes that a person has the reputation of being good while he is unknown, but his presence darkens the eyes of those who see him. We seek to please by our companionableness. Instead we cause displeasure by the fickleness people see in us.

CHAPTER NINE

Obedient Submission

It is excellent to live under obedience to a superior and not to be on our own. It is much safer to be in a position of submission than to be a superior for others. There are, however, many who are under obedience from necessity rather than from personal choice. They find obedience awkward and are quick to grumble. They will not achieve proper mental freedom until they submit themselves completely for God's sake. Wherever you search you will find peace only in humble submission to the guidance of a superior. Yearning for other places and for change has disappointed many.

Each of us seeks the company of like-minded people and does willingly what he finds pleasant. Yet, if God is in us, we have at times to ignore our own preferences for the sake of harmony. Who can be so wise as to know everything? Do not, therefore, trust too much to your own feelings. Seek more awareness of the feelings of others. Even if what you feel is good, and you, in God's name, disregard this and follow the wishes of another, greater perfection will be yours.

I have often heard it said that it is safer to listen to

and accept advice than to give it. It can happen that each one's opinion is well-founded; but to be unwilling to give way to others, when occasion and reason demand it, is a sign of prideful stubbornness.

CHAPTER TEN

Avoiding Gossip

As far as possible, avoid the chatter of men; for even well-intentioned discussion of worldly affairs is a distraction. Frivolity soon soils and captivates us. Often I should have been silent and have avoided men. Why should we chatter and talk carelessly? The return to silence always brings the prick of conscience. The aim of our careless chatter is to seek pleasant human contact and to lighten a heart heavy with many wants. We are anxious to discuss what is nearest our hearts and to complain about what hurts us.

Yet, alas! Our conversation is often pointlessly vain. Outward comfort such as this is no small obstacle to divine inward solace. Pray diligently, therefore, that your time may not be spent in idleness. If speech is necessary and required, speak only what is constructive. Bad habit and lack of zeal for perfection make us very careless in our speech.

Serious discussion of the things of the spirit is indeed a great help towards spiritual maturity, especially among those of like minds and ideals, who live together under God.

CHAPTER ELEVEN

Peace and Progress

We can attain great peace if we are unwilling to busy ourselves with the doings and sayings of others that are none of our concern. How can a man stay at peace when he is fuddled with other peoples' worries, when he busies himself over public concerns and is seldom or never inwardly composed? Happy the simple: they possess great peace.

Why were some of the saints so perfectly composed? They strove to deaden in themselves all desire for earthly things: thus they were able to empty themselves at will and hold fast to God with the very marrow of their hearts. We are too busied with personal ambition and seek too anxiously after what passes away. We overcome hardly one vice, we fail to achieve even ordinary perfection and we remain coldly lukewarm.

If we were perfectly dead to ourselves and less wrapped up in ourselves, then we could reach out to the divine and have even a little experience of heavenly contemplation. The greatest obstacle of all is that we are not liberated from our own ambitions and wants. We do not even try to follow the example of the saints. We are dejected even at the slightest difficulty and turn in search of human solace.

If we strove to stand firm like brave men in battle, then surely we would see God's help reach out to us from heaven. He is ready to help those who try hard and trust in his grace. If our idea of perfection centres round only the outward observances of religion, our enthusiasm will soon dampen. But if we get down to the basics and purge our ambitions, then we will possess a truly peaceful mind.

We would be perfect indeed if each year we were to root out one vice. But, more often than not, we find that we were better and more sincere in the beginning of our conversion than we are now, after many years of profession. Our fervour and progress should have increased daily; yet now it seems a great achievement if anyone retains even a little of his first fervour. If we had made the slightest effort in the beginning, then the things that came afterwards could have been achieved with pleasant ease.

It is hard to conquer habit and even harder to go against one's own inclinations. But, if in small and insignificant matters you do not succeed, how will you solve more difficult problems? Resist your inclinations in the beginning and root out the habit that will perhaps lead you little by little into greater difficulty. If you realised the peace to yourself and the pleasure to others that your self-control brings, I think you would be more anxious to achieve spiritual perfection.

CHAPTER TWELVE

Adversity's Usefulness

It is good for us now and then to experience difficulties and adversity; for they make man realize again that he is an exile and should not put his hopes on any worldly thing. It is good too that we should be contradicted and ill-thought of, even when we act with the best intentions. Experiences like these help us towards humility and guard us against vainglory. When outwardly we are slandered and ill-thought of, then we will yearn more anxiously for God's inward witness.

We should, therefore, be so firmly united to God that there is no need for us to hanker after human consolations. When a well-disposed man is disturbed or tempted or afflicted with evil thoughts, he understands how great is his need for God. He can achieve so little by his own efforts. At such a time of sadness and tears he prays about the trials he suffers. He wearies of life and yearns for death as a means *of being dissolved and being with Christ* (Phil 1: 23). At such a time he realises well that perfect security and peace are not to be found in this life.

CHAPTER THIRTEEN

Control of Temptation

So long as we are in this world we cannot be long without temptation. Thus in Job it is written: *Is not man's life on earth nothing more than pressed service?* (Job 7: 1). So each man should be wary of temptation and never cease to pray in case the sleepless devil *prowling round like a roaring lion* (1 Pet 5: 8) should find opportunity to trip him. No one is so perfect or so holy as not to be tempted sometimes. We can never lack temptations entirely.

Often enough temptations are helpful to a man,

even though they may be tiresome and uncomfortable. Man is purified by them. They teach him humility. All the saints progressed and reached perfection through many trials and temptations. Men who were unable to resist temptation became sinners and fell away. There exists no order so holy nor any place so remote as to be without temptations and difficulties.

Man, as long as he lives, is not safe from temptations; for the source of temptation, our passions, with which we were born, is within us. From the time that we lost original happiness, when one temptation goes another takes its place. There is always something to be suffered. Many seek to escape some temptations, but fall more grievously into others. Flight alone will not bring us victory. We will achieve strength only through simple patient humility.

If a man resists temptations on the surface only and fails to uproot them, he will make little progress. He will return to them more quickly and feel all the worse. With God's help we can achieve better control gradually and with careful patience. Harsh self-nagging does no good. Be quick to take advice when tempted and do not deal harshly with anyone who is tempted. Be as kind to him as you would have him be to you.

The root of all evil temptations is a certain inconstancy of purpose and lack of trust in God, like a rudderless ship buffeted about by the waves. The careless and inconstant man is tempted in different ways. Fire tries iron. Temptation tries the just man. We do not often realise our capacities. Temptation shows us what we are. We must be especially careful when temptation begins; for it is easier to overcome

the enemy if he is forbidden entry into the mind.
Meet him therefore at the threshold where he knocks.
Therefore someone has said:

> *In the beginning stand firm, too late comes the*
> *medicine*
> *When illness weakens by its long remaining . . .*
> (Ovid: De Remediis, II, 91)

First comes the simple thought, then strong attrac-
tion, afterwards delight, improper desire and assent.
Thus gradually the wicked enemy comes into us, if
he is not resisted at the outset. The longer one puts
off resisting the weaker one becomes daily and stronger
the enemy against us.

Some have more serious temptations in the beginning of conversion, and some at the end. Some are
afflicted throughout their lives. Others again are but
lightly tempted. This is no doubt because of the
wisdom and mercy of God's providence. He measures
up the particular strength of each man and arranges
everything for the safety of his chosen ones.

We should not, therefore, give up hope when we
are tempted, but all the more fervently plead with
God to help us in every trial. For St Paul tells us *with*
any trial he will give you a way out of it (1 Cor 10: 13),
so that you can bear it. Let us, therefore, in every
temptation and trial, place ourselves humbly in God's
care; for the *Lord will rescue the just man* (Ps 33: 19).
He will raise him up.

Through temptations and trials a man is tested as
to how greatly he has progressed; through them he
gains much merit and his virtue shines out the more
clearly. It is indeed no wonderful thing that a man is

fervent and holy when he experiences no great hardship, but, if he is patient in time of trial, then he shows great hope of progress. Some are preserved from great temptations, but daily succumb to little ones so that, humbled, they do not put too much trust in themselves; for they realise their weakness in such trifling matters.

CHAPTER FOURTEEN

Avoiding Rash Judgement

Mind your own business and avoid judging the actions of others. Judging others, a man gains little profit, is often mistaken and easily offends. He does, however, gain much profit from judging and examining himself. Often we judge matters in accordance with what we always want. Influenced by pet prejudice, we lose right judgement. If God was always the simple object of our longing, then we would be less easily disturbed by opposition to our opinions.

We are often drawn along by hidden internal motives and also by outside happenings. Many, quite unconsciously, seek only themselves in whatever they do. They seem quite contented so long as matters go according to their wishes and opinions; but, let things go contrary to their wishes, and they are quickly distressed and upset. Often enough dissensions between friends and neighbours, between the religious and the devout, arise from differences of sentiment and opinion.

Old habit dies hard, and nobody is easily led beyond

what he himself can see. If you put your trust in your own understanding and efforts more than in the subduing power of Christ, enlightenment will come to you slowly and perhaps not at all. It is God's will that we be perfectly subject to him and that our whole mind be filled with burning love.

CHAPTER FIFTEEN

Charitable Works

An evil deed may not be performed either for worldly benefit or for love of any man; but, for the benefit of the needy, a good work may be interrupted or perhaps changed for a better one. In this manner a good deed is not destroyed, but is transformed into a better. Any outward act which lacks charity is valueless; but whatever is done out of charity, be it ever so small or insignificant, becomes fully fruitful. For God measures not so much the deed as how great is the motivation for the deed.

He who loves much achieves much. He who does anything well achieves much. He does well who serves the common good rather than his own wants. Often what appears to be love is simple lust. For natural inclination, self-will, hope of reward and love of convenience are seldom absent.

He who possesses really perfect charity seeks personal benefit in nothing; but his whole desire is to realise the will of God in all matters. Caring neither for private pleasure, nor even for the joy of self-respect, he chooses to be absorbed in the blessedness of God, the supreme good. He envies no man. He attributes good to no man and refers everything to God, the fountain of all good, in whom all the saints reach final rest. Were a man to have but a spark of perfect charity, then he would realise that all earthly things are but vanity.

CHAPTER SIXTEEN

Suffering Others' Faults

A man must put up patiently with those things in himself and in others, which cannot be corrected until such time as God orders things differently. Think of them rather as tests of our patience, without which our progress might be of little value. Nevertheless, when you are bothered by such things, it is right and proper that you should ask God's aid in putting up with them.

Do not quarrel with a person, even if he fails after one or two warnings to be accommodating. Put everything in God's hands so that his will may be realised in all his servants. He knows indeed how to convert evil into good. Seek always to be tolerant of the shortcomings and failings of others. They also have much to tolerate in you. If you are unable to mould yourself as you wish, how can you expect others to conform to your liking? Though quick to expect perfection in others, we take little care to correct our own shortcomings.

We would have others strictly corrected, but not ourselves. The wide freedom of others displeases us;

yet we wish to be denied nothing that we ourselves desire. We would have others under the restraint of the rule while unwilling ourselves to be under any sort of restraint. Thus it is evident that we rarely regard our neighbour as our equal. If everybody was perfect, then we would have little to suffer from others for the sake of God.

It is God's plan that we should learn to *carry each other's troubles* (Gal 6: 2). There is no one free of faults, no one burdenless, no one self-sufficient, no one clever enough to stand alone. We must support one another, comfort one another, help build up one another by instruction and advice. The strength of one's virtue is seen more easily when opposition comes. For such opposition does not weaken a man, but shows his mettle.

CHAPTER SEVENTEEN

Life in the Monastery

To achieve peace and harmony with others you must learn to control yourself in many ways. It is no small matter to live in a monastery or in a community, to remain there without rancour and faithfully to persevere there until death. Happy the man who has lived and persevered there happily and well. To maintain steadfast progress you should regard yourself as an exile and a pilgrim on this earth. To lead a religious life you should become a fool for Christ's sake.

The habit and the tonsure are of small importance. It is the change in life style and the complete giving up of one's own wishes that make the true religious. He who seeks anything other than God alone and his own salvation will find nothing but trial and sorrow. He who does not strive to be the least and the most subdued will not remain at peace for long.

You have come to work, not to organise. Know that you are called to suffer and to work, not to be idle and not to gossip. Here men are tried as gold in the furnace. No one can stay here unless he is willing to humble himself totally in the service of God.

CHAPTER EIGHTEEN

The Example of the Holy Fathers

Consider the vivid examples of the holy fathers in whom the true perfection of religion shone out, and you will realise the smallness and insignificance of our efforts. Alas! What is our life compared to theirs? Holy friends of Christ, they served the Lord in hunger and thirst, in cold and nakedness, in labour and fatigue, in fasts and vigils, in prayer and contemplation, in many persecutions and slanders (cf 2 Cor 11: 27).

O the number and the greatness of the trials suffered by the apostles, martyrs, confessors, virgins and all those others who sought to follow in the footsteps of Christ. They hated their souls in this life so that they might possess those souls in eternal life. O what a severely self-denying life was led by the holy fathers in the desert! What long and serious trials they underwent! How often they were vexed by the enemy! How frequent and fervent the prayers they offered to God!

How strict was their abstinence! How great their burning zeal for spiritual perfection! How strongly they waged war against the tyranny of vices! How pure was their single-minded yearning for God! They laboured by day, prayed the night long and even when working hardly ever interrupted their mental prayer.

They used every moment well. Every hour in God's service seemed but a moment. In the very pleasure of contemplation they were forgetful of the body's need for rest. They gave up wealth, position, glory, even friends and relatives. They sought to have nothing worldly and took only the bare necessities of life. They were unhappy even in illness to serve the body. They were poor indeed in the earth's goods, but immensely rich in grace and virtue. Outwardly they were destitute, but inwardly they were sustained by divine grace and solace.

They were strangers in the world, but close and fast friends of God. They thought little of themselves and were despised by the world, but they were precious and beloved of God. They stayed in simple humility; they lived in simple obedience; they walked in patient charity; at the same time they made spiritual progress and gained great grace with God. They are set before us as an example to all religious. They should spur us to make good progress more than the host of the lukewarm (that would tempt us) to laxity.

O how fervent were religious institutes in the early days of their foundation! How devoted were their prayers! How great their search for virtue! How firm was their discipline! How reverently and obediently, in accordance with the Master's rule, they acted in everything! The ruins they left behind witness the holy perfection of those who strove so valiantly to crush the world underfoot. Nowadays a man is regarded as great if he has not broken the rule, if he has managed patiently to tolerate his lot.

How negligently tepid is our state of life, so ready to drop away from first fervour, so bored, so unenergetic and so tired of life! How is it that progress in virtue is almost asleep in you when you have seen so many examples of devotion?

CHAPTER NINETEEN

Religious Exercises

The life of the good religious should be strong in every virtue, and he should be inwardly just as he appears outwardly to men. Indeed his inner qualities should be greater than what is seen on the surface. For our examiner is God whom we must always revere, wherever we may be, and in whose sight we should walk like angels. Each day we should reaffirm our commitment and rouse in ourselves such fervour as if only today we had been converted. Daily we should pray: Strengthen, Lord, my commitment to your holy service and grant that I should begin this day perfectly; for my past deeds have been as nothing.

The rate of our progress depends on our commitment. The man who wishes to make good progress needs great application. If indeed a man of strong commitment fails sometimes, what will happen to the man who rarely or with less strong purpose makes his resolve? There are many ways by which we give up our commitment. Even the omission of a small exercise entails some sort of loss. The resolve of good men is dependent more on God's grace than on personal cleverness. In God they always place their trust, come what may. Man indeed proposes, but it is God who disposes *nor is the course of man in his power as he goes his way* (Jer 10: 23).

If a customary exercise is omitted by reason of piety or because of fraternal concern, later recovery may be easy. But if such an exercise is carelessly omitted out of negligence or boredom, that is a fault which will prove harmful. Even though we strive hard we will easily be found lacking in many things. Nevertheless, we must constantly make firm resolutions, especially against those things which hinder us most. We must examine carefully both our outward and inward devotions; both help us to progress.

If you are unable to keep your mind constantly on God, try to gather your thoughts at least once per day, either in the morning or in the evening. In the morning, make resolutions; in the evening, examine what you have done regarding the day's words, deeds and thoughts. In these matters it is likely that you have offended God and your neighbour. Gird yourself like a man against devilish evils. Curb over-eating and control of your other bodily appetites will be easier. Never be entirely idle; either read or write or pray or meditate or work for the common benefit. But be careful in the performance of bodily exercises; not everybody needs the same amount of exercise.

Non-community exercises are not to be publicly performed; such exercises as are private are, for safety's sake, to be carried out quietly. Be careful that you are not slow to attend community exercises and overkeen on private devotions. When you have faithfully and completely fulfilled all that the rule requires, then you may give yourself to private devotion. Not everybody can manage the same exercises. For one this devotion is helpful, for another a different devotion is more suitable. At different times too, different exercises are suitable. Some are more suitable to festivals and others to ordinary days. Some exercises are suited to times of trial, others to times of peace and solace. We like to think of some things when we are sad and others when we are happy in the Lord.

At the time of great festivals, good exercises should be repeated. At such times the intercession of the saints is to be fervently implored. We should make our resolutions from festival to festival as though we were about to leave this world and come to the eternal festival. At such times of devotion, we should prepare ourselves carefully. We should be more devout in our conversation. We should pay stricter attention to each observance as if we were soon to receive God's reward for our labours.

And if that day of reward is delayed, trust that it is so because we lack preparation. We are as yet unworthy of that glory which will be revealed to us at the appointed time. Strive then to make better preparations. *Happy that servant* (says St Luke the evangelist) *if his master's arrival finds him at his employment: I tell you solemnly, he will place him over everything he owns* (Mt 24: 47 and Lk 12: 37).

CHAPTER TWENTY

Desire for Quiet Solitude

Frequently seek a suitable time to consider the good things God has done. Avoid curious matters and study such things as will help move you to repentance, and not simply pass the time. If you avoid unnecessary talk and idle wandering about, and do not listen to news and gossip, you will be able to spend enough time in suitable meditation. As far as they could, the greatest of the saints avoided human company and preferred to serve God in secret.

It has been said: *As often as I have been with men I have returned less a man.* (Seneca, Letters 7). We experience this often when we gossip too long. To remain entirely silent is easier than not to talk too much. To stay quietly at home is easier than trying sufficiently to guard oneself abroad. A man who chooses the inward and the spiritual should remove himself with Jesus from the crowd. No one goes abroad with safety who is not willing to stay quietly at home. No one speaks out with safety who is unwilling to hold his tongue. No one governs with safety who is unwilling to be governed. No one gives commands with safety who has not learned well how to obey.

No one rejoices with safety unless he is sure that his conscience is clear. The security of the saints, however, was always Godfearing and they were no less concerned about humility, in spite of being recognised as such good holy people. The security of the wicked arises from great pride and presumption. In the end it turns to self-deception. Never promise yourself security in this life, even though you may seem to be a good monk and devout hermit.

The highest in men's esteem are often in the gravest danger because of overconfidence. For many, therefore, it is safer that they should not be entirely free of temptation, but constantly harassed in case they become too secure or lifted up with pride or too easily reach out for outward comfort. If a man could cut out all empty care and think only of salutary and divine matters, what a great peace and solace would he possess!

No one is worthy of heavenly consolation unless he has tried hard to achieve holy repentance. If you wish to have deep-hearted sorrow, go into your room and shut out the noise of the world. As it is written, *Spend your night in quiet meditation* (Ps 4: 5). You will find in your room what is often lost outside. The room a man keeps to becomes sweet; the room that is not kept to generates boredom. If in the beginning of your religious profession you keep to your room and guard it well, it will become your special friend and most pleasant solace.

The devout soul makes progress in quiet and in silence. She learns the hidden lessons of the scriptures. There she discovers gushing tears that nightly wash and cleanse her. She draws closer to her Maker the more she withdraws herself from the clatter of the world. God and his angels come closer, therefore, to the man who withdraws himself from friends and acquaintances. It would be better for a man to have quiet care for himself than to neglect himself and work wonders. It is praiseworthy in a religious person to go out seldom, to avoid being seen and even to be unwilling to see other men.

Why do you wish to see what you may not have? *The world and all its cares is coming to an end* (1 Jn 2: 17). Desires for satisfaction of the senses may persuade you to walk abroad; but, when the hour is past, what have you to show for it but a certain heaviness of conscience and distraction of heart? A joyful departure gives birth often to a sad return. A merry evening makes for a sad morning. Every pleasure of the flesh begins pleasantly, but in the end bites and destroys. What do you see outside that you cannot see here? You have the sky, the earth and the elements. Everything is made of these.

Where can you see anything that shall remain long under the sun? You expect perhaps a satisfaction that is always just beyond your reach. If you were to see everything before you, would it not be but an empty dream? *Lift your eyes to God who has his home in heaven* (Ps 123: 1), and pray about your sins and omissions. Leave vain matters to the vain and pay attention to those things that God has placed in front of you. *Shut your door* (Mt 6: 6) and summon Jesus your beloved. Stay with him in your room. You will not find such peace elsewhere. If you had not gone out and listened to idle gossip you would have stayed in more perfect peace. Your delight in hearing news must sometimes make you suffer anxiety of heart.

CHAPTER TWENTY ONE

Heartfelt Repentance

If you wish to make any progress, remain Godfearing

and do not be too easy going. Discipline all your senses and do not give yourself to frivolous mirth. Practise yourself in heartfelt sorrow and you will find devotion. Sorrow reveals the beauty that frivolity generally destroys. If a man considers and weighs up his exile state and the dangers to which his soul is subject, the wonder is that he can be glad at all in this life.

Light-hearted lack of concern for our faults dulls our appreciation of the soul's sorrows. We laugh foolishly when, by rights, we should weep. True freedom and gladness do not exist apart from a good Godfearing conscience. Strive manfully. Habit is overcome by habit.

If you know how to leave men alone it is well that you leave yourself alone to get on with your work. Do not busy yourself with the concerns of others nor meddle in the business of your betters. First, scrutinise yourself. Carefully criticise yourself, not those you love. If you are not popular, do not be upset, but consider it a serious matter that you do not behave as well and as circumspectly as a servant of God and devout religious should. It is often better and safer that a man should lack many of the satisfactions of this life, especially the satisfactions of the flesh. Yet, if we lack and experience but seldom the satisfaction of divine things, we have ourselves to blame. For we have not tried hard to achieve heartfelt sorrow. We have not renounced entirely all vain outward comforts.

Realise that you are unworthy of divine consolation and more worthy of tribulation. When a man is perfect in repentance the whole world is burdensome and bitter to him. A good man always finds enough cause for sorrow and for weeping. If he considers himself or examines his neighbour he realises that nobody alive is without troubles. The more strictly he examines himself the more he sorrows. Our sins and vices, which so hamper us that we rarely achieve divine contemplation, are the ground for our just regret and deep sorrow.

If you think of your death more frequently than of the length of your years, there is little doubt that you will strive more sincerely for improvement. If you meditate on the future pain of hell and of purgatory, I believe that you will be willing to suffer toil and sorrow. No rigour will scare you. But because these thoughts hardly cross our minds and we still love passing pleasures, we remain very coldly slothful.

Often it is for want of spirit that the wretched body complains so easily. Pray humbly, therefore, that God may give you the spirit of repentance and say with the prophet: *Feed me with tears for my bread and abundance of tears for my drink* (Ps 79: 5).

CHAPTER TWENTY TWO

Man's Unhappiness

You are unhappy wherever you are, wherever you turn, unless you commit yourself to God. Why be upset that you do not experience the success you wish and desire? Is there anyone who has everything the way he wants? Neither I nor you nor anyone on earth. Nobody in this world is without trial or restriction, be he King or Pope even. Who then is better off? Only the man who manages to suffer something for God.

Many of the weak and foolish exclaim: What a good life so-and-so has! How rich! How great! How powerful and exalted! But, consider heavenly things and you will see how all such matters are as nothing. They are very uncertain and especially burdensome in that they necessarily involve a certain amount of worry and fear. The gladness of man is not in having a lot of worldly possessions. Enough is enough. Life on earth is sad indeed. The more a man seeks to be spiritual the more bitter his present life becomes, in so far as he sees better and is more clearly aware of the frailities of human corruption. Dependence on the necessities of nature, eating, drinking, waking, sleeping, resting, working, this is an unhappy affliction to the devoted man who yearns to be unloosed and free from sin.

The inward person is greatly burdened by bodily necessities in this world. The prophet therefore begs devoutly to be released from them. He says: *Free me from my necessities, O Lord* (Ps 24: 17). But woe to him who does not know his own misfortune. Woe even more to such as actually love the corruptible misery of this life. They are so wrapped up in it that, if it were possible, they would be content always to stay here and ignore the kingdom of God, even though by labour and begging they can hardly get together the necessities of life.

How foolish and how faithless of heart are those who are so completely involved in earthly things that all their wants are of the flesh. How wretched they will be when they come to the sad realisation of how base and worthless were the things they loved. The saints of God and all Christ's devoted friends cared little for what pleases the flesh or what prospers at the present time. All their trust and yearning was for goods that are eternal. Their whole desire was carried upwards to those unseen goods that are stable. Their fear was that they might be dragged down by the love of things that are seen. Brother, do not lose hope of making spiritual progress while you still have time.

Why do you wish to postpone your commitment? Get up, begin immediately, and affirm: This is the time for action. This is the time to fight. The time is now ripe for improvement. When you are ill and suffering, then is the time to gain merit. The way to refreshment is through fire and water. You will not conquer vice unless you make an effort. So long as we carry about this frail body we cannot be without sin nor live without weariness and sorrow. We would be glad to be entirely free of care; but, because we have lost original innocence through sin we have also lost true happiness. Therefore we should be patient. We should trust in God's mercy until such time as iniquity passes away and mortality gives place to life.

How great is human weakness, always inclining to evil. Today you confess your sins and tomorrow you do again what you confessed. Now you resolve to be careful and within an hour you act as though you had made no resolution. With good reason, therefore, we can think little of ourselves and regard ourselves as of no great importance. We are very frail and unstable. We can easily lose by carelessness what was barely achieved through grace and great effort.

What will become of us in the end, who are so quick to lose fervour? Woe to us if we choose to rest as if peace and security had already arrived, even though our conversation gives no evidence of even the first sign of true sanctity. It would be better if we were like good novices being taught how to acquire good habits. Then perhaps there might be some hope of improvement and spiritual progress.

CHAPTER TWENTY THREE

Thoughts of Death

Soon enough you will be finished with this life. Consider therefore how things will stand with you in the next: today a man is and tomorrow he is gone. When he has been removed from our sight he is soon out of mind as well. O the dullness and the hard heartedness of man that he considers only what is present and has not more thought for the future! You ought to behave in thought and in deed as if you were about to die. If your conscience is clear you have not much to fear in death. It is better to steer clear of sin than to fear death. If you are not ready today how will you be ready tomorrow? Tomorrow is an uncertain day. How do you know you will have a tomorrow?

What is the value of a long life if we improve so little? A long life does not always bring improvement, but often piles up more faults. Would that we had spent even a single day well in this world. We can count many years of profession, but often with poor results in improvement. Death may be fearsome; perhaps long life is more dangerous. Happy the man who keeps the hour of his death always before his eyes and every day is ready to die. When you see another man die remember that you too must pass that way.

In the morning consider that you might not last till evening. In the evening dare not promise yourself the morning. Be prepared always. Live in such a way that death will never find you unready. Indeed *The Son of Man is coming at an hour you do not expect* (Lk 12: 40). When that last hour comes you will begin to have a different opinion of your past life. You will regret your past negligence and carelessness.

Happy and sensible is the man who seeks to be in this life just as he would choose to be found in death. The things that will give you great hopes of happiness in death are: perfect disregard for the world, zeal in pursuit of progress and virtue, love of discipline, self-denial and suffering adversity for the love of Christ. While you are healthy you can achieve much; but while you are sick I do not know what you can achieve. Sickness brings reform to very few; and seldom are many made holy by repeated pilgrimages.

Do not trust in friends or neighbours. Do not put off your salvation to the future. Men will forget you sooner than you realise. It is better now to make provision and store up good ahead of time than to put your trust in the prayers of others. If you do not look after yourself now, who will look after you hereafter? Now is the most precious time. These are *the days of salvation, the favourable time* (2 Cor 6: 2). But what a pity that you do not use this time more usefully to gain merit for eternal life! There will come a time when you will beg a day or an hour to repent, and I do not know whether you will get it.

Dearly beloved, if always you have reverent thoughts of death, from what dangers can you be freed, from what terror saved? Strive to live now in such a way that in the hour of death you will be glad rather than fearful. Learn to die to the world now so that then you can begin to live with Christ. Learn to despise all now so that then you can be free to go to Christ. Discipline your body with penance now so that then you may have sure and steadfast confidence.

Foolish one, why do you hope for long life when not even one day is certain? How many there are who think they will live long, but are mistaken and snatched from the body unexpectedly. How often have you heard it said: This man fell by the sword; that man was drowned; another fell and broke his neck; yet another was taken while at table and the other was at sport when the end came. One by fire, another by steel, yet another by pestilence and again another by thieves met his death. Death is the end of all men and man's life is a shadow that quickly passes by.

Who will remember you after your death? Who will pray for you? Do, do now, beloved, what you can. You do not know when you will die nor do you know what will happen to you after your death. While you have time gather up imperishable riches. Think only of your salvation; care only for the things of God. Make friends now by honouring the saints and imitating their deeds. When you leave this life, *they will welcome you into the tents of eternity* (Lk 16: 9).

Act like a pilgrim and a guest on the earth. Ignore the business of the world. Keep your heart free and upstanding in God's sight. Here you have *no eternal city* (Heb 13: 14). Direct your daily prayers and tearful sighs in such manner that your soul may earn a passage to the Lord.

CHAPTER TWENTY FOUR

Judgement and Punishment

Consider the end of all things and how you will stand before that strict judge from whom nothing is hidden. He is uninfluenced by bribes and listens to no excuses. He will judge strictly according to justice. O wretched fool of a sinner! How will you answer to God, the knower of all evil? Now you fear even the scowl of an angry man. How shall you provide against the day of judgement when no man will be excused or defended by another, but each will be fully occupied defending himself? Now your effort is fruitful, your tears acceptable, your cries attended, your sorrow cleansing and redemptive.

The patient man has a wholesome purgatory. For, suffering injury, he bewails the malice of others more than the wrong done to himself. He is ready to pray for his opponents, is quick to forgive and is willing to ask for forgiveness. He is more merciful than irascible. He submits himself to vigorous discipline and strives to subject his flesh entirely to the Spirit. It is better to purge sin and prune vice now than to wait for purification at some future time. Our misdirected affection for the things of the flesh really deceives us.

What else will that fire feed on but your sins? The more gentle you are with yourself, the more you follow the flesh, the harder it will be for you when later you will provide more fuel for the fire. Each man will be punished according to the nature of his sins. The indolent will be goaded with burning spurs, the greedy crucified with great thirst and hunger. The lovers of conspicuous luxury will be mired in burning pitch and stinking sulphur; the envious, like wild dogs, will howl with frustration.

No vice will be without its particular torment. The proud will be covered in shame. The greedy will be held down by miserable want. There one hour's punishment will be heavier than one year's penance here. There will be no rest, no respite for the damned. Here and now there is at least a little rest from work, some friendly solace to be enjoyed. Work hard at repenting your sins so that you may be safe among the blessed on the day of judgement. *The virtuous man stands up boldly to face those who have oppressed him* (Wis 5: 1) and ground him down. Then he shall stand at the judgement who now submits himself to the judgement of men. Then the poor and the humble will have great confidence and the proud will be surrounded with fear.

Then the one who has learned to be despised and to be a fool for Christ will seem to have been worldly wise. Then all the trials patiently borne will be cause for pleasure and *wickedness must hold its tongue* (Ps 107: 42). Then all the committed will be glad and the irreligious shall sorrow. Then the stricken flesh shall rejoice more than that which has been pampered with delights. Plain clothes shall sparkle and fine vesture lose its brightness. Then the poor man's simple hut will be valued above the gilded palace. Then patient constancy will be of greater worth than worldly power. Then simple obedience will stand high above worldly wisdom.

Then shall more joy rise out of a good simple conscience than out of clever philosophy. Then contempt for wealth will weigh heavier than all earthling treasure. Then you will rejoice more in the devotedness of your prayers than in the delicacy of your diet. You will rejoice the greater for silence maintained than for gossip sustained. Then will holy deeds be of more value than many fair words. Then strictness of life and severity of penance will please more than all earthly delight. Learn now to suffer a little so that then you will be freed from heavier problems. Test first here what you can manage hereafter. If you can suffer so little now, how will you manage to suffer eternal torment? If a little pain irks you now, what will hell do to you? Indeed you cannot have pleasure both ways, earthly delight here and reigning with Christ hereafter.

If up till this moment you had lived in luxury and glory, what good would it do you if you happened to die at this moment? All is vanity except to love God and to serve him alone. He who loves God fears neither death nor punishment, nor judgement nor even hell. For perfect love secures our approach to God. It is no wonder that he who loves sin fears death and judgement. If love does not draw a man from sin, it is good that at least fear of hell force him from it. The man who leaves God's love on one side can hardly remain good. He easily falls into the devil's snares.

CHAPTER TWENTY FIVE

Reforming our Lives Completely

Be constantly watchful in God's service and consider

frequently: Why have I come here? Why did I leave the world? Surely it was to live for God and become a spiritual person? Be ardent therefore for progress. You are soon to receive the reward of your labours and fear and sorrow shall no longer invade you. For a little labour now you will discover great peace and gladness. If you persevere ardently in faithful deeds, God will certainly be faithful in generously rewarding you. You must be steadfast in your hope of achieving victory, but it is not fitting that you feel too secure for fear you become slothful or over-confident.

There was once a man who wavered so much between fear and hope that he was almost overcome with worry. He came once to a church and knelt in prayer before the altar, repeating over and over again: I wish I knew if I would persevere or not. Suddenly he heard within himself the divine reply: What would you do if you knew this? Do now as you would do then and you will be safe enough. Consoled and comforted, he soon submitted himself to God's will. His anxious wavering ceased. He lost his anxious desire to inquire about his future and strove only to know God's beneficent and perfect will in the matter of good works to be started and to be completed.

Trust in the Lord and do what is good. Make your home in the land and live in peace (Ps 37: 3). One thing pulls many back from progress and ardent improvement: a loathing for the difficulty and effort of striving. I assure you that those who strive manfully to overcome what they find difficult and obnoxious achieve greater virtue than others. Indeed a man makes better progress and gains greater grace when he overcomes himself and disciplines his spirit.

Not everyone has the same amount to overcome nor needs the same amount of discipline. Even though he be very passionate, the man who works hard will achieve greater perfection than another who is well behaved, but less ardent for virtue. Two things are special helps towards improvement: forceful withdrawal from nature's evil tendencies and ardent striving towards the virtue which is most lacking. Strive also to escape and overcome whatever you find offensive in others.

May you grasp at every opportunity for progress. Where you see or hear good example may you be stirred to follow it. When you notice any deed worthy of condemnation, take care that you do not do likewise; and if you do so sometimes, try to correct yourself as quickly as possible. Just as you see others so also you are seen by them. How sweet and pleasant it is to see brothers fervent and committed, well-behaved and well-disciplined. How sad and unpleasant it is to see gadabouts who fail to do what their vocation requires of them. How harmful it is when they ignore their calling and meddle in what is none of their business.

Remember the commitment you have accepted and keep the example of the crucified before you. If you consider the life of Jesus Christ, you have reason for shame. For, though long on the way to God, you have not yet modelled yourself sufficiently on Jesus. The religious person who reflects with devout attention on the most blessed life and sufferings of the Lord finds there in full measure all that he needs to use. He need not search further than Jesus. If the crucified Jesus would come into our hearts, how quickly and how fully would we be instructed.

The ardent religious bears himself well and does what he is bid. The careless religious experiences trial upon trial and suffers restriction on all sides; he lacks interior solace and is prevented from seeking solace outside. A religious who does not live according to the rule will suffer serious harm. If he seeks laxity and exemptions, he will always be in distress. There will always be one thing or another to upset him.

How do so many other religious fare who are sufficiently restrained by discipline and cloister? They go out seldom. They lead a retired life. They eat poorly. They dress simply. They work hard. They speak little. They watch late. They rise early. Their prayers are long, their reading frequent and they keep all the rules. Consider the Carthusians and the Cistercians and many other such religious orders of monks and nuns. They rise in the middle of the night to praise the Lord in psalms. It would therefore be shameful if you were held back by sloth from such a holy task by means of which such a multitude begins to rejoice in God.

Would that you had nothing else to do but praise the Lord God. Would that you need neither eat nor drink nor sleep so as to be able to praise God and concern yourself with what is spiritual. Then you would be happier than ever you are when you serve the different needs of the body. Would that these needs did not exist and we had only the taste for spiritual satisfaction.

When a man has reached the stage that he seeks no creature comfort, then he begins really to know God. Then he is content with whatever befalls. Then neither does he rejoice over great things nor does he worry over little things. He places himself with complete trustfulness in God's hands. God is everything to him. To God nothing dies or passes. Everything lives and immediately serves his will.

Always remember your end and the passing loss of time. You will not acquire virtue without some care and effort. If you begin to cool, you begin to do ill. If you give yourself to fervour, you will find great peace. Every effort will seem easier because of God's grace and the strength of your love. A diligently ardent man is ready for everything.

It is more laborious to resist vice and passion than to sweat in bodily labour. If you do not avoid small faults, you will soon commit greater ones. You will always rejoice in the evening if you spend the day well. Watch yourself, stir yourself, counsel yourself and, no matter what others do, do not neglect yourself. The greater effort you take, the greater will be your progress.

Amen.

BOOK TWO

THE LIFE THAT IS INWARD

CHAPTER ONE

What is the Inward Life?

The Kingdom of God is among you, says the Lord (Lk 17: 21). Turn wholeheartedly to the Lord. Leave the misery of this world and your soul will find peace. Learn to despise what is external and to embrace what is interior. You will discover thus that God's kingdom will come to you. God's kingdom is not given to the ungodly. It is *peace and joy brought by the Holy Spirit* (Rom 14: 17). If you make ready within yourself a proper resting place, Christ will come to you and show you his comfort. His glory and beauty are all within. He finds pleasure there (cf Ps 44: 14). Often he visits the true seeker for holiness to share with him quiet pleasant comfort, deep peace and really close companionship.

Faithful soul, make your heart ready to meet this bridegroom whenever he decides to come and visit you. For he says: *If anyone loves me he will keep my word . . . and we shall come to him and make our home with him* (Jn 14: 23). Find room for Christ, but keep all others out. When you possess Christ, you are rich and content. He will be your provider and faithful guardian in everything. No need to rely on men. Men indeed are very quick to change and too ready to desert. *The Christ*, however, *remains for ever* (Jn 12: 34), and always stands firm.

Put no great trust in weak or mortal man, no matter how useful or pleasant he may be. We should not be over sad when men oppose us sometimes and contradict us. Today they are with you, tomorrow against you. Often they swing right round like the wind. Put your whole trust in God. Let your fear and your love be centred in him. He will care for you and will do for you what is best. *There is no eternal city for us in this life* (Heb 13: 14). Wherever you are, you are a stranger and a pilgrim. You will not find even passing peace, except in union with Christ.

Why do you search about in this place where you can find no rest? *Your dwelling place should be in heaven* (2 Cor 5: 2). You should view all earthly things as one who simply passes by. All things pass, and you as well. See that you remain detached lest you are caught and perish. May your thoughts be always on the most High, your humble ceaseless prayers directed to Christ. If you lack the ability to meditate on high heavenly things, seek comfort in the sufferings of Christ. Be content to gaze on his sacred wounds. Take refuge in Christ's wounds and in the marks of his passion. There you will feel great comfort in times of sorrow. You will put little value on men's disrespect. You will pay little heed to what those who slander you say.

Even Christ was despised on earth. When he needed help most and was condemned on all sides, he was deserted by his friends and acquaintances. Christ chose to suffer and be despised. Why then do you dare complain about anybody? Christ had enemies and opponents. Why do you expect all men to be your friends and wellwishers? What reward can you gain by patience, if you experience no opposition? If you are unwilling to suffer opposition how can you be Christ's friend? Suffer with and for Christ, and you may reign with Christ.

Would that even once you had sunk yourself in Jesus. Would that you had felt even a little of his burning love. Then you would care little for your convenience or inconvenience. You would rejoice even in the reproach you suffer. The love of Jesus makes a man think little of himself. If a man really loves Jesus, if he really seeks holiness, if he is free from undisciplined affection, then he can turn freely to God, raise himself up in the spirit and enjoy peace.

A man who sees things as they are, not as they are said or thought to be, is a wise man. God, not men, is the source of his learning. A man who can walk in holiness ignores external things. He does not have to search around for a place or a suitable opportunity for devout prayer. He gathers his thoughts quickly. He does not waste energy on external things. Outside work or such casual tasks as are necessary are not obstacles for him. He takes things as they come. If a man is well disposed and disciplined in his approach to interior things, he cares little for the astonishing oddity of what men sometimes do. Man is hindered and distracted just in so far as he makes himself the centre of everything.

If you were really cleansed, then everything would help your progress to perfection. The reason why you feel such displeasure and annoyance is that you are neither dead to yourself nor detached fully from earthly things. Nothing so soils and confuses a man as impure love of creatures. If you renounce external comfort, you will be able to contemplate heavenly things. Frequently you will experience inward joy.

CHAPTER TWO

Humble Submission

Whatever you do, do not think which man is for or against you. Let your care and concern be whether God is with you. If your conscience is good, God will support you. Nobody's malice will hurt a man whom God has chosen to help. If you can suffer in silence, you will certainly enjoy God's help. He knows when and how to free you. Put yourself in his care. It is for God to aid us and free us from uncertainty. Often greater humility is preserved in us when others know and condemn our shortcomings.

A man who is humble about his faults pleases others. He easily satisfies those who are angry with him. God guards the humble man and sets him free. He loves him and comforts him, he grants him great grace, he transforms his humiliation into glory. He reveals his secrets to the humble man and draws him to himself with gentle persuasion. A humble man may suffer great shame, but he is at peace. For he trusts in God rather than in the world. Consider that you have made no progress at all until you recognise that you are lower than everybody else.

CHAPTER THREE

The Peaceable Man

Be at peace yourself. Then you will be able to bring peace to others. The peaceable man gets more good done that does the learned man. The passionate man turns even good into evil. He is ready to believe evil. The good peaceable man makes everything good. The man that is really at peace suspects nobody. The troubled discontented man is torn apart with suspicions. He is neither at peace himself nor will he let others be at peace. Often he says what he should not say and fails to do what he should have done. He counts the obligations of others and ignores his own obligations. First, correct yourself strictly. Then, with some justification, you can be strict in correcting others.

You are well able to excuse and condone your own actions; but you are unwilling to accept the excuses of others. You would be more just if you accused youself and excused your brother. If you want to be put up with, put up with others. Think how far away you are from real charity and from that humility which can be angry and indignant with nobody but yourself. Living with good gentle people is no great trial. Naturally everybody finds this pleasant. Every man likes peace and loves those who agree with him. But to be able to live peacefully with those who are perverse and stubborn, ill-tempered and cantankerous, that requires great grace and is praiseworthy behaviour, worthy of a man.

Some people are at peace with themselves and keep

peace with others. Others are not at peace with themselves and will not let others be at peace. These are a burden to others and an even greater burden to themselves. Some keep themselves at peace and strive to bring peace to others. Nevertheless, our peace in this unhappy life is from humble endurance, not from the absence of opposition. The more a man can suffer, the more he is at peace. He gains self-control, power over the world, friendship with Christ and the right to inherit heaven.

CHAPTER FOUR

Purity and Simplicity

Simplicity and purity are the two wings that raise a man above earthly things. He must have simplicity of desire and purity of affection. Simplicity directs man to God; purity grasps God and tastes him. You will find no good deed a burden if you are inwardly free of undisciplined desire. If your end and aim is for nothing but God's will and the good of your neighbour, you will enjoy inward freedom. If you had the right attitude, you would see every creature as a mirror of life and a book of holy teaching. There is no creature so small and unimportant that it does not reflect the goodness of God.

If you were inwardly pure and good, you would see everything clearly and understand all. A pure attitude penetrates heaven and hell. A man's inward attitude is shown by his outward judgements. Any joy there is in this life is possessed by the man whose attitude is pure. Any trial and worry anywhere is known best by those whose consciences are evil. Iron in the fire loses its rust and becomes all bright. In the same way, a man who turns totally to God casts off his laziness and becomes a new man.

When a man begins to lose fervour, he fears even a little effort and gladly seeks outward comfort. When he starts to control himself fully and begins to walk along manfully with God, he regards as unimportant what before he regarded as burdensome.

CHAPTER FIVE

Self-Esteem

We cannot depend too much on ourselves. Often we lack grace and understanding. For a short time we have some insight, but quickly lose it through carelessness. Often we are quite unaware of our inward blindness. By excusing ourselves we add to the evil of our deeds. At times we are prompted by excitement and mistake it for zeal. We are critical of small faults in others, but ignore our own greater defects. We are quick to weigh and tally what we suffer from others, but pay no heed to the amount others suffer from us. A man who judged his own deeds well and rightly would find no justification for judging others harshly.

The inward man puts self-control above all other aims. If a man examines himself carefully he finds it easy to be silent about others. To achieve inward commitment you should keep silent about other men and look specially to your own business. If your whole concern is for yourself and for God you will be affected little by what you see around you. If you are not in touch with yourself, where are you? To have seen everything has done you little good if you have neglected yourself. To possess peace and real union you must concentrate on yourself and put everything else aside.

You will make great progress if you keep yourself free of all worldly concern. You will fall back if you set high value on any worldly thing. Let nothing except God alone or what is of God be great, high, pleasant or acceptable to you. Regard any comfort as empty if it comes from any created thing. The soul that loves God despises all that is less than God. God alone is eternal and unbounded, filling everything. He is the soul's comfort and the heart's delight.

CHAPTER SIX

The Joy of a Good Conscience

The glory of a good man comes from the knowledge that his conscience is true. Keep a good conscience and you will have lasting joy. A good conscience is strong in endurance and joyful in adversity. A bad conscience is always fearful and worried. You will rest comfortably if your heart does not condemn you. Rejoice only when you do good. The wicked indeed never really find enjoyment. They never have even a taste of peace. *There is no happiness, says Yahweh, for the wicked* (Is 48: 22).

If they say: We are at peace; evil does not come to

us; who dares hurt us? do not believe them. Suddenly God's anger will flare up, their deeds will be reduced to nothing and their plans will collapse.

The lover does not find it burdensome to glory in troubles. For so to glory is to glory in the cross of the Lord. The glory that men give and take is short-lived. Sadness always walks hand in hand with the glory of the world. Good men rejoice in the goodness of their conscience, not in the good opinion of men. The joy of the just is from God and in God. Truth is their pleasure. He who seeks lasting glory has no care for worldly things. The seeker after earthly glory, who does not distrust it deeply, shows little love for heavenly glory. A man who cares neither for praise nor for condemnation enjoys great calmness of heart.

A man whose conscience is pure easily acquires peace and contentment. You are not more holy because you are praised. You are not meaner because you are slandered. What you are you are. You can say no more than that you are God's witness. If you pay attention to what you are inwardly, you will not worry about what people say concerning you. *Man looks at appearances, but Yahweh looks at the heart* (Is 16: 17). Man looks at what is done. God weighs the motivation. To do good always and to think little of oneself is the mark of a humble soul. To be loth to accept the comfort of any created thing is a sign of great purity and inward confidence.

A man who does not rely on what people say about him shows that he has committed himself totally to God. *It is not the man who commends himself* (says the Blessed Paul) *that can be accepted, but the man who is commended by the Lord* (2 Cor 10: 8). To walk

inwardly with God and to be caught by no worldly
attachment is the way an inward man lives.

CHAPTER SEVEN

Love Jesus above all

Happy the man who understands the love of Jesus and
knows how to despise himself for Jesus' sake. You
should give up what you love for the one you love.
Jesus wants to be loved above all. A creature's love is
false and inconstant. Jesus' love is faithful and firm.
He who clings to a creature will fall as it falls. He
who clings to Jesus will stand firm for ever. Love him
and hold him as a friend who, when all others desert
you, will never leave you and never let you perish.
Whether you like it or not, you have to leave everyone
sometimes.

Stay with Jesus, alive or dead, and trust yourself to
him with confidence. When all others have left you,
he alone is ready to help. Your beloved is such that he
wishes to exclude any stranger, to possess your heart
entirely and to sit there as king on his own throne. If
you can be detached from every creature, Jesus must
gladly stay with you. All that you have entrusted to
men, and not to Jesus, will be lost. Neither trust nor
lean upon a wind-shaken reed. For *all flesh is grass,
and its beauty like the wild flower's* fades (Is 40: 6).

If you observe only men's outward appearance, you
will be quickly deceived. If you seek comfort and
profit in others, you will often discover loss. If you
seek Jesus in all things, you will find Jesus. If you

seek yourself, you will indeed find yourself, but also your own destruction. If a man does not seek Jesus, he does himself more harm than the whole world and all his enemies can do him.

CHAPTER EIGHT

Close Friendship with Jesus

When Jesus is present, everything seems good and nothing difficult. When Jesus is absent everything is hard. When Jesus does not speak to us inwardly, we have little comfort. But, let Jesus speak just one word and our sense of satisfaction is great. Did not Mary Magdalen get up immediately from where she wept when Martha said to her: *The Master is here and wants to see you* (Jn 11: 28)? O happy time when Jesus calls you from tears to joy in the spirit! How dry and stiff you are without Jesus! How foolish and vain you are to seek anything beyond Jesus! To do this would mean greater loss than if you were to lose the whole world.

If you are without Jesus, what can the world give you? To be without Jesus is a burdensome hell; to be with Jesus is sweet heaven. If Jesus is with you, no enemy can harm you. The finder of Jesus discovers in him a fine treasure, a good above every good. He who loses Jesus loses much indeed, more than the whole world. He is poorest who lives without Jesus; he is richest who stays well with Jesus.

To know how to talk with Jesus is a great skill. To know how to hold fast to Jesus is great wisdom. Be humble and peaceable. Jesus will be with you. Be quietly devout. Jesus will stay with you. If you turn aside to give your attention to outward things, you can easily flee Jesus and lose his grace. If you lose him, if you flee from him, to whom shall you turn and whom shall you seek for a friend? You cannot live without friends. If Jesus is not your best friend, you will be lost and sad indeed. You act foolishly, therefore, if you place your trust or seek pleasure in anyone else. You should choose, therefore, rather to have the whole world against you than to offend Jesus. Let Jesus be the most specially loved of all that are dear to you.

All are to be loved for Jesus' sake, but Jesus for his own sake. Jesus alone is to be loved specially; for he alone above all friends is known to be good and true. Through him and in him let enemies be as dear as friends to you. You must pray that all may love and serve him. Do not seek to be specially praised or loved. Such praise belongs only to God to whom none is equal. Do not desire that any man should set his heart on you. Do not set your own heart on any man. Let Jesus be in you and in every good man.

Be pure and inwardly free of any attachment to created things. You must give God a pure naked heart if you wish to understand how good the Lord is. Indeed you cannot achieve this unless his grace goes before you and pulls you on. Then, emptied of all and having left all, you can achieve union with him alone. God's grace coming into a man makes him able to do any-thing. When it goes, it leaves him poor, weak and like one waiting to be whipped. If this happens, he should not become dejected or hopeless, but stand quietly, awaiting God's will. He should put up with everything that comes about for Jesus' praise. After winter comes summer, after night comes day, and after each storm the calm.

CHAPTER NINE

When Comfort is Absent

When divine comfort is present it is not difficult to ignore human solace. It is, however, a very great thing to be able to lack comfort both human and divine, to be willing to suffer loneliness for the glory of God, to seek yourself in nothing and to ignore personal benefit. Joyful commitment is no heavy task when grace is at hand. Everyone likes times like these. To ride on God's blessings is nice enough. Borne by the Almighty and guided by the Supreme Leader, the absence of any sense of burden is no great surprise.

We are happy to seek comfort. But it is difficult for a man to strip himself of himself. The holy martyr, Lawrence, and his priest conquered the world by despising whatever the world thought desirable. He was happy to let even his best friend, Sixtus the Bishop, be taken away from him. He overcame his human love by the love of the Creator. You too should learn to leave close loved friends for the love of God. When friends leave you, do not take it amiss. You know we must all be parted sometime.

A man learns complete self-control and aims all his desires at God only after long and serious self-discipline. A man who relies on himself will easily slide back towards human comfort. The real lover of Christ and the earnest seeker of virtue does not slide back into such comforts. He does not hanker after the pleasures of the senses. Instead he seeks to undergo stiff trials and hard labour for Christ's sake.

When divine comfort is granted, take it with thanks; but realize that it is a gift from God and that you do not deserve it. Do not be too cocky. Do not be too glad or too sure of yourself. Regard the gift as a reason for humility. Let it make you careful and reverent in whatever you do. Such times will pass and temptation will come. When comfort is gone, do not lose hope. Wait with humble patience for that heavenly visit by which God can give back to you an even greater comfort. Those with experience of God will find nothing novel or strange in this. The greatest of the saints and the prophets of old often had this experience of opposites.

The Psalmist said, therefore, when grace was near: *In prosperity I used to say: Nothing can ever shake me* (Ps 30: 6). When grace was absent, he speaks of his experience thus: *Then you hid your face and I was terrified* (Ps 30: 7). Yet he does not despair on account of these experiences. He pleads earnestly with the Lord: *Yahweh, I call to you, I beg my God to pity me* (Ps 30: 8). Finally he speaks of the benefit of his prayers and witnesses that he has been heard. He says: *The Lord has listened to me. He has taken pity on me. The Lord has become my helper* (Ps 30: 10). How did this come about? You have turned my mourning into dancing, he says . . . *and wrapped me in gladness* (Ps 30: 11). If such is the experience of great saints, such weaklings as we should not give up hope when we blow hot and cold by turns. The Spirit comes and goes as it wishes. Therefore, Job says: *What is man . . . that morning after morning you should examine him and at every instant test him?* (Job 7: 18)

On what, therefore, can I depend? What should I trust besides God's mercy and blessing? You may enjoy the company of good men, of committed brothers or of trusted friends. You may have holy books and beautiful treatises, fine chants and hymns. All these are small helps. When grace is absent and I am left to my own poor devices, they have but little taste. Then, patient surrender to God's will is the best medicine.

I have never met anyone of such religious commitment that he never felt some lessening of grace or cooling of fervour. No saint was ever so upright or enlightened that he was not tempted sometimes. Unless a man has been tested by trial, he is not worthy of high godly contemplation. *Those who prove victorious*, it is said, *I will feed from the tree of life* (Rev 2: 7).

Divine comfort is given to a man to strengthen him in time of adversity. Temptation comes to him to stop him being proud of the good he has received. The devil never sleeps. The flesh is not yet dead. Never, therefore, be unprepared for battle. Enemies that do not rest are about you.

CHAPTER TEN

Gratitude for God's Grace

You are born to labour. Why then do you want rest? Be ready to suffer rather than to be comforted, to carry the cross rather than to enjoy gladness. Anybody on earth would be glad to get spiritual joy if he could always have it. Spiritual comforts are greater than any worldly delight or bodily luxury. All worldly delights are either foolish or filthy. Spiritual delights alone are pleasant and proper. They rise out of goodness and are poured by God into pure minds. While temptation lasts, however, no man can enjoy at will such divine comforts.

False freedom of spirit and too great trust in self are obstacles to heavenly contact. When God gives the grace of comfort, he does well. When man fails to return everything with thanks to God, he does ill. Thus the gift of grace cannot flow through us because we are ungrateful to the source and do not pour all back into the fountainhead. Grace indeed is always due to the grateful. What is given often to the humble is withdrawn from the proud.

I do not wish comfort if it will banish repentance. Nor do I wish contemplation if it leads to pride. Not all that is high is holy. Not all that is pleasant is good. Desire is not always pure. Not all that is cherished pleases God. Gladly I accept grace so that I can become more reverently humble and more ready to deny myself. A man taught by the gift of grace, who has learned the lesson given by the shock of its withdrawal, dares not depend only on himself. He is more prepared to admit that he is poor and naked. Give to God what is God's and to yourself what is yours; that is, give thanks to God for his graces and know that you deserve only such punishment as fits your guilt.

Take the lowest place and you will be given the highest. There can be no highest without a lowest.

The saints that God loved the greatest were those who thought the least of themselves. The humbler they felt, the more glorious they were. Filled with truth and heavenly glory, they wanted no empty show. Firmly grounded on God, they could not be proud. Those who attribute everything to God seek no praise for themselves, no matter what good they receive. They desire only that praise which is God's. They wish only that God be praised in himself and by all his saints. This is what they strive after constantly.

Be grateful, therefore, for even the littlest and you will be worthy to receive the greatest. Think of the least as the greatest and judge the thing worthy of the greatest contempt as a special gift. Think of the dignity of the giver and no gift will seem mean or poor, especially if it is given by God most high. God is due thanks even when he gives us punishments and beatings. Whatever he lets happen to us is always done for our salvation. The man who wants to remain in grace should give thanks for every grace that is given. He should be patient when grace is taken away. He should pray that it comes back and be fearfully humble lest he loses it again.

CHAPTER ELEVEN

The Lovers of the Cross

There are many lovers of Jesus' heavenly kingdom, but few who will carry his cross. There are many who wish for comfort, but few who wish for trial. Jesus finds many to eat with him, but few to fast with him.

Many want to rejoice with him, but few wish to suffer anything for his sake. Many follow Jesus in the breaking of bread, few in drinking the chalice of his sufferings. Many admire his miracles, but few share the shame of his cross. Many love Jesus so long as no difficulties stand in the way. Many praise him and bless him so long as he comforts them. When Jesus hides himself and puts himself at a distance for a while, then they become querulous and dejected.

There are those who love Jesus for Jesus' sake, not for personal comfort. These bless him as their greatest comfort in time of trial and distress. Yet, even if he did not agree to grant them comfort, they would still praise him and always thank him.

The simple love which is not mixed with self-interest or self-love is great indeed. Those who are always anxious for consolation deserve to be called hirelings. Are not those who are always after comfort and convenience evident self-lovers, not Christ-lovers? Can anyone be found anywhere who would serve God for nothing? You will rarely find a man so spiritual as to be stripped of everything. Can you find any man so poor in spirit as to be stripped of all possessions? *She is far beyond the price of pearls* (Prov 31: 10). When a man gives away all his property it is nothing. When he does severe penance it is still very little. He may know everything, but still be off course. Even if he achieved great virtue and ardent devotion, something would still be lacking: namely, what he needs most. And what is this? He must give up everything, including himself. He must get outside himself totally and keep within himself nothing that belongs to self-love.

When he has done all that he knows must be done, he should still think himself worthless.

Let him not value as great what can be thought great. Let him really admit that he is a worthless slave. For Truth says: *When you have done all that you have been told to do, say: 'We are merely servants'* (Lk 17: 10). In this way he can be really poor and naked in spirit and he can say with the prophet: *alone and wretched as I am* (Ps 25: 16). No man is richer, more powerful, more free than he who can leave all and take the lowest place.

CHAPTER TWELVE

The Royal Way of the Cross

Renounce yourself, take up your cross and follow Jesus (cf Mt 25: 41). To many this seems *intolerable language* (Jn 6: 61). It will be harder, however to hear as final sentence: *Go away from me with your curse upon you, to the eternal fire* . . . (Mt 25: 41). A man who is willing to listen and who carries out the words of the cross need not be afraid of hearing a sentence of eternal damnation. The sign of the cross will be in heaven when the Lord comes to judge. Then all those servants of the cross, who have modelled themselves on him who was crucified, will come forward with confidence to Christ, their judge.

Why are you afraid to carry the cross? It leads to the kingdom. In the cross there is safety, life, and protection against foes. In the cross there is a flood of heavenly sweetness, strength of mind, joy of spirit, the greatest virtue and perfection of holiness. Only in the cross will the soul find either salvation or hope of everlasting life. Carry your cross, therefore, and follow Jesus to everlasting life. He went ahead of you, carrying the cross. He died for you on the cross. You too can carry the cross. You too can desire death on the cross. If indeed you have died with him, you shall also live with him. If you share his suffering, you will also share his glory.

Look at it this way. Under the cross everything stands together, under death all is laid out. There is no other way to life and to inward peace except by dying daily to oneself in the way of the holy cross. Wherever you go and whatever you seek, you will not find a higher road above nor a safer road below than the way of the holy cross. Arrange and order matters as you like or as you think they ought to be. You will discover that there is always something to be suffered, whether you like it or not. You will always come back to the cross. Either you will feel bodily pain or you will suffer mental anguish.

Sometimes God will forsake you. Sometimes your neighbour will upset you. What is worse, you will often be a burden to yourself. You will be unable to find any remedy or solace to release you and ease your pain. You must suffer as long as God wills it. God wishes you to learn to suffer trial without comfort. He wants you to submit yourself and through trials to learn humility. No man understands the sufferings of Christ so well as the man who has had to suffer the like. The cross is for ever present and always waits on you. Wherever you run, you cannot escape it. You carry yourself wherever you go. You will always be there. Turn yourself over and under and inside out; you will always find the cross. Everywhere and always, you have to be ready to suffer if you wish to reach eternal peace and the eternal crown which has been promised.

If you are glad to carry the cross, it will carry you to the end you seek beyond this place, where suffering shall cease. If you are unwilling to carry the cross, you build yourself a burden that increases your weariness and has to be borne all the same. If you throw off one cross you will certainly find another, and perhaps a heavier one.

Do you think that you can escape what no mortal man has ever been able to avoid? Which saint on earth was ever without trial or the cross? So long as he lived, not even Jesus Christ was without suffering. *Was it not ordained*, it is written, *that Christ should suffer, rise from the dead and so enter his glory?* (Lk 24: 26 & 24: 46) Why then do you seek a road that is different from the royal path which is the way of the cross?

Christ's whole life was a cross and a martyrdom. Why then do you seek only rest and pleasure? You are mistaken, mistaken indeed if you expect anything but suffering and trials. This whole life is full of unhappiness and is sealed over with crosses. The greater spiritual progress a man makes, the heavier crosses he will find. For the pain of separation increases with the growth of love.

Nevertheless, when a man is afflicted like this in many ways, he finds some easing comfort. He understands the great benefit that comes from supporting his cross. So long as his submission is willing, all the burden and trial is transformed into sure hope of divine comfort. The more the flesh is restrained by affliction, the greater is the strengthening of the spirit by inward grace. Sometimes a man is so anxious to be modelled on the cross of Christ and so strong in his desire for trial and opposition, that he does not wish to be without trial and suffering. The more acceptable he believes they make him in God's eyes, the greater his capacity for accomplishing more and greater things. It is not so much the man's strength as the grace of Christ that can and does use weak flesh to achieve so much. Warmth of spirit can make a man embrace and love what is naturally to be avoided as abhorrent.

Carrying the cross is not pleasant for a man. It is not easy to love the cross, to beat the body into submission, to flee honours, to be happy to suffer shame, to despise oneself and choose to be despised, to suffer adversity and loss and to look for no worldly prosperity. Examine yourself. You can achieve nothing like this on your own. If you trust in God, strength will be given to you. The world and the flesh will be obedient to your word. Armed with faith and signed with the cross of Christ, you will fear no devilish enemy.

Like a good trusted servant, get yourself ready manfully to take the weight of the cross on which your lord was crucified for you. Be prepared to suffer great adversity and inconvenience in this sad life. They will be your lot, wherever you are, and you will find them, wherever you hide. This is how things have to be. There is no way of escaping the trials of evil and sorrow. We have to put up with them. Drink lovingly of the Lord's chalice if you desire to be his friend and partner. Leave comfort to the Lord. Let him do what he pleases about it. Get yourself accustomed to putting up with trials. Think of them as the greatest comforts. *What we suffer in this life can never be compared to the glory as yet unrevealed* (Rom 8: 18), even if you had to suffer everything yourself. When trial for Christ's sake becomes sweet to you and tastes good, you may think that all is well. You have found heaven on earth. So long as you find suffering burdensome and flee from it, things will go badly for you. You will try to avoid every trial.

If you set yourself to do what you have to do, to suffer and to die, things will soon go better for you and you will find peace. Even if, like St Paul, you were lifted up to the third heaven, you would not, because of that, be safe from suffering adversity. *I myself will show him*, says Jesus, *how much he himself must suffer for my name* (Ac 9: 16). If you wish to love Jesus and serve him always, you must suffer.

Would that you were worthy to suffer something for Jesus' name! How great would be the glory that awaits you! How great would be the saints' rejoicing! How good an example to your neighbour! Everybody praises patience, but few are willing to practise it. You have good reason to be glad to suffer a little for Christ's sake. Many suffer more burdensome things for the world's sake.

Know for sure that you should lead a dying life. The more a person dies to himself, the more he begins to live in God. No one can grasp heavenly things unless he accepts adversity for Christ. Nothing is more acceptable to God, nothing more wholesome for you on earth than to suffer gladly for Christ. If the choice is yours, you had better choose to suffer adversity for

Christ than to enjoy great comfort. This would make you more like Christ, a truer model of his saints. Our merit and progress does not depend on our having great sweetness and comfort, but rather in putting up with great difficulties and trials.

If there was a way better and more suitable than the way of suffering, then Christ would have shown us it by word and example. Christ clearly exhorts the disciples that followed him and all those who wanted to follow him to carry the cross. He said: *If anyone wants to be a follower of mine, let him renounce himself and take up his cross and follow me* (Mt 16: 24). To all then that we have read and studied let this be the final conclusion: *We have to experience many hardships before we can enter the kingdom of God* (Ac 14: 22).

BOOK THREE

INWARD COMFORT

CHAPTER ONE

Christ's Inward Conversation with the Faithful Soul

The Servant: I am listening. What is the Lord saying?
(Ps 84: 8). Happy is the soul who listens to the Lord
speaking to her. She receives words of comfort from
his mouth. Happy are the ears that catch the drift of
the divine whisper and ignore the whisperings of the
world. Happy that clear hearing which does not heed
the noise of the outside world, but attends to the
inward voice that teaches truth. Happy those eyes that
are closed to outward things and open to what is
inward. Happy are those who understand what is
inward. By daily prayer they seek to make themselves
more and more ready to grasp the secrets of heaven.
Happy are those who try very hard to empty themselves for God and cut themselves off from every
worldly hindrance. Note this, my soul. Shut the door
on your passions. Let yourself hear what your Lord
God says to you.
   The Lord: Your beloved speaks: *I am your salvation*
(Ps 35: 3), your peace and your life. Stay with me and
you will find peace. Leave what is passing. Choose the
everlasting. What are the things of time but deceits?
If the creator leaves you, what good can any created
thing do for you? Leave everything. Make yourself

pleasing to your creator. Then you may be able to grasp true happiness.

CHAPTER TWO

The Wordless Voice of Truth

The Servant: Speak, Yahweh, your servant is listening (1 Sam 3: 10). *I am your servant. If you will explain, I will embrace your decrees* (Ps 119: 25). *Turn my heart to your decrees* (Ps 119: 36). *May your teaching fall like rain* (Deut 32: 2). Formerly, the children of Israel said to Moses: *Speak to us yourself and we shall listen; but do not let God speak to us, or we shall die* (Ex 20: 19). Lord, I do not wish to pray like that. I would rather follow the example of the prophet Samuel and beg you: *Speak, Yahweh, your servant is listening* (1 Sam 3: 10). Let neither Moses nor any prophet speak to me. Better you, Lord God who inspires and enlightens every prophet, you speak to me. Without them you alone can fill me up perfectly. Without you they can do nothing.

They can mouth the words, but do not instil the spirit. Their words are beautiful. Yet, if you are silent, they do not set the heart on fire. They deliver the letter. You unfold the meaning. You unlock the hidden meaning of the mysteries they proclaim. You help man carry out the commandments they reveal. You give strength to walk the road they point out. Their work is outward only. You teach and enlighten the heart. They water the outside. From you comes the gift of fertility. They shout words. You grant understanding of what is heard.

Do not let Moses speak to me; but you, O Lord, my God and Truth Eternal, speak to me for fear I become dead and barren, only outwardly instructed and not inwardly on fire. Do not let me be judged because I heard the word and did not do it, understood the word and did not love it, believed the word and did not keep it. *Speak, therefore, Yahweh, your servant is listening* (1 Sam 3: 10). *You have the message of eternal life* (Jn 6: 69). Speak to me. My soul will be comforted. My life will be improved. May you yourself be praised, glorified and honoured always.

CHAPTER THREE

Listen Meekly to God

The Lord: Son, listen to my words. They are very pleasant. They go beyond all the knowledge of the philosophers and sages. *The words I have spoken to you are spirit and life* (Jn 60: 63). They are not to be judged as men think. They must not be used for empty comfort. Listen to them in silence. Accept them very lovingly and meekly.

The Servant: I have said: *Yahweh, happy the man whom you instruct, the man whom you teach through your law; his mind is at peace when times are bad* (Ps 93: 12–13).

The Lord: I taught the prophets in the beginning. Up till now I have not ceased speaking to everyone. Yet many are obstinately deaf to my voice. Many listen more gladly to the world than to God. They would rather follow the lust of the flesh than the will of God. The world promises poor passing benefits and is served with eagerness. I promise what is great and everlasting and the hearts of men are indifferent. Is there anyone who would serve and obey me with as much effort as is spent on the service of the world and its lords? *Blush, Sidon, for thus speaks the sea* (Is 23: 4). And, if you want a reason, here is why. For a little gain men run a long way. To gain eternal life they will not lift a foot once from the ground. They go after mean advantage. Sometimes they cheat and haggle over one coin. They are ready to work night and day for some foolish little promise.

They are too lazy to make the slightest effort to gain the good that does not change, the reward that cannot be measured, the honour and glory that is beyond all limit. Blush then, you lazy bickering servant. Others work harder for perdition than you do for life. They take greater pleasure in appearances than you do in the truth. Often enough they are disappointed. Yet, if anyone trusts in me, my promise will not fail him or disappoint him. I grant what I have promised. I do what I have said. A man need only persevere faithfully in my love. I am the rewarder of every good, the strong prover of all that are committed.

Write my words on your heart and think about them carefully. In time of temptation, you need them very much. I visit those whom I love in two ways, by temptation and by comfort. Daily I read them two lessons, the one condemning their vices, the other exhorting them to increase in virtue. Anyone who hears my words and rejects them will be judged on the last day.

PRAYER: Lord, my God, you are every good I have. Who am I that I should dare to speak to you? I am the

poorest of your servants, a grovelling worm, poorer
and much more contemptible than I know or dare to
say. Remember, Lord, that I am nothing, I have nothing and I have no worth. You alone are good, just and
holy. You can do everything. You give everything.
You fill everything and leave only the sinner empty.
Remember your kindness (Ps 25: 6) and fill my heart
with grace. You do not wish that your deeds should
become void. How can I persevere in this miserable
life if your kindness and grace do not strengthen me?
Do not turn your face away from me. Do not prolong
your punishment. Lord, do not take away your comfort
for fear my soul becomes to you *like thirsty ground*
(Ps 143: 6). Lord, *teach me to obey you* (Ps 143: 10).
Teach me to live worthily and meekly in your presence. You are my wisdom. You know me well. You
knew me before the world was and before I was born
into the world.

CHAPTER FOUR

Living the Truth with God

The Lord: Son, walk with me in truth. Seek me always
in the simplicity of your heart. A man who walks
with me in truth will be safe from every evil attack.
The truth will free him from those who tempt him
and from the slanders of the wicked. If the truth frees
you, you will be free indeed. You will care nothing
for men's empty words.

   The Servant: What you say is true, Lord. I wish to
be like that. Let your truth teach me. Let it guard me
and, in the end, bring me to salvation. Let it keep me

from evil desire and from undisciplined love. Let me walk with you in great freedom of heart.

The Lord: Truth says: I will teach what is right and pleasing to me. Examine your sins with sorrow and grief. Never think highly of yourself because of your good deeds. You are indeed a sinner, wrapped in many offensive lusts. Your own efforts are worthless. You are quick to fall, quickly defeated. You are quickly troubled, quick to give up. You have no cause for pride and much reason for being condemned. You are weaker than you understand.

Do not, therefore, think highly of yourself because of what you do. Count nothing great, valuable, admirable or worthy of fame, nothing high, praiseworthy or desirable except what is everlasting. May your greatest pleasure be everlasting truth, your own great meanness your constant disgust. Fear nothing, condemn nothing, flee nothing so much as your own vices and sins. They should cause you more sorrow than any other loss. Some indeed follow me with insincerity. Moved by pride and curiosity, they want to know my secrets and understand the depths of God; but they neglect their own salvation. I stand against such people. Pride and curiosity makes them liable to great temptation and to sin.

Fear the judgements of God and tremble before the wrath of the almighty. Do not spend your time studying the works of the most high. Study your own wickedness, the greatness of your faults and the amount of good you have left undone. The devotion of many is centred on books, pictures, images and external signs. Many have me on their lips, but not in their hearts.

Others have minds that are enlightened and hearts that are pure. They yearn always for what is everlasting. Hearing about earthly concerns bores them. They do not want even to care for the necessities of nature. They understand what the spirit says to them. It teaches them to despise earthly things, to love heavenly things, to ignore the world and, night and day, to yearn for heaven.

CHAPTER FIVE

The Wonders of Divine Love

The Servant: Heavenly Father, Father of our Lord Jesus Christ, I bless you for your tenderness in thinking of one so poor as me. Father of Mercy, God of all comfort, I thank you for the refreshing comfort you give me. I am not worthy of any comfort at all. I bless and glorify you for ever, together with your only Son and the Holy Spirit, the comforter. O Lord, my holy loving God, when you enter my heart, my whole inside heaves with joy. You are the glory and joy of my heart. You are my hope and *shelter when I am in trouble* (Ps 59: 17).

I am weak in love and imperfect in virtue. So I need your strength and comfort. Come to me often. Instruct me in holy knowledge. Free me from evil lust. Cure my heart of all undisciplined love. Cure me inwardly. Purify me and make me able to love. Make me strong in suffering and firm in perseverance.

The Lord: Love is a great matter, the greatest of good things. It makes light what is heavy. It makes everything equal. It carries burdens without effort. It makes sweet and tasty all that is bitter. The noble love of Jesus urges great achievements and rouses constant desire for perfection. Love surges upwards and is held down by nothing base. Love goes forward to freedom. It is a stranger to such worldly desire as might block its inward vision, cause entanglement in passing good fortune and make it downcast by misfortune. There is nothing in heaven or earth so sweet as love, nothing so strong, nothing so high, nothing so broad, nothing so pleasant, nothing so full and nothing so good. For love is born of God. It can find fulfilment only in God above all created things.

The Lover floats and runs with joy. He is free and unbound. He gives all for all and owns all in all. He finds fulfilment in the one, highest above all, from whom all goodness flows and comes out. He does not care about the gift, but turns his attention first and foremost to the giver. Love seldom bothers about measure and boils over beyond measure. Love feels no burden, weighs no effort. It strives to do more than it can. For love impossibility is no excuse. It thinks that it can and may do everything. Love, therefore, does everything. The lover manages to achieve things that would cause the non-lover to falter and collapse.

Love is watchful. Asleep, it does not slumber. Tired, it is not weary. Bound, it is not restrained. Afraid, it is not upset. It is like a dancing flame, a burning torch that flares up and finds its way in safety. The true lover knows what I mean. Burning spiritual love is a shout in the ear of God, that announces: You are my love, my God. You are all mine and I am all yours.

The Servant: Expand my love that I may learn to

relish with the heart's inward palate the sweetness of loving. Let me melt and bathe in love. Let me rise above myself in warmth and wonder, embraced in love. Let me sing a song of love. Let me go with the beloved to the height. Let my soul gasp with the praise and joy of love. Let me love you more than me, myself only because of you. Let me love all true lovers because of you. The law of love, shining out of you, ordains it so.

The Lord: Love is swift, sincere, pious, pleasant and delightful. It is strong, silent, patient, trustful and wise. It is tolerant. It has a manly disregard for personal profit. The self-seeker fails in love. Love is careful, humble and right. It is neither soft nor frivolous. It is unconcerned with what is foolish. It is sober, chaste, stable, content and disciplined in all matters of the senses. Love is demure and obedient to superiors. It has a low opinion of itself. Gratefully committed to God, it trusts and hopes in him, even when he grants no taste of himself. A man cannot live love without some sorrow.

You are unworthy to be called a lover because you are not ready to suffer everything and give up your own will for the sake of the beloved. A lover should embrace all that is difficult and bitter for the beloved. He should not turn aside from the beloved, no matter what difficulty comes.

CHAPTER SIX

Recognising True Love

The Lord: Son, you are not yet a strong and prudent lover.

The Servant: Why, Lord?

The Lord: A little opposition makes you stop what you started. You are too greedy for comfort. The strong lover stands fast in the face of temptations. He puts no trust in the clever arguments of the enemy. I please him when things go well. I please him also when things go badly.

The prudent lover considers not so much the lover's gift as the love of the giver. He looks at the love that gave the gift rather than the cost. He places the beloved above all. The noble lover takes pleasure not in the gift, but in me above every gift. All is not, therefore, lost if at times your feelings for me and for the saints are less pure than you would wish. That good pleasant feeling you have sometimes is a result of the grace that is in you. It is a sort of foretaste of the heavenly homeland. Do not become overconcerned about this feeling. It comes and goes. To fight against evil intentions that are aroused in the soul, to spurn the devil's persuasion, these are signs of strength and great merit.

Do not be disturbed by weird imaginings, no matter where they come from. Be firm and direct your mind straight to God. You are not mistaken when you feel at times a sudden great uplift and just as sudden return to your usual emotional weakness. You put up with these unwillingly. You do not bring them about. So long as you regard them as unpleasant and worrisome, there is merit in them and no loss.

Know this. The old enemy tries hard to frustrate your desire to do good and to turn you away from all practice of prayer and from thoughts that are worthwhile. He tries to make you lift the guard that is on your heart and to deflect you from your resolve to make progress in virtue. He pushes you towards many evil thoughts in order to make you bored and timid. He calls you away from prayer and holy studies. He dislikes your humble confession. If he were able, he would make you give up holy communion. Do not trust him. No matter what deceitful traps he sets for you, ignore him. When he suggests the evil or the vile, accuse him of it. Say to him: Be off, vile spirit. Blush for shame. You are a filthy fellow to turn my ears to such as this. Leave me, wicked deceiver. Keep out of my way. Jesus like a strong warrior will be with me. You will be defeated. I would rather die and suffer any punishment than agree with you. *Silence now! Be quiet!* (Mk 4: 39). I will listen to you no longer, though you wear me down with interference. *Yahweh is my light and salvation, whom need I fear* (Ps 27: 1)? *Though an army pitched camp against me, my heart would not fear* (Ps 27: 3). *Yahweh is my rock and my redeemer* (Ps 19: 14).

Fight like a good soldier. If sometimes your weakness causes you to fall, rejoin the battle with greater efforts than before. Trust in the fullness of my grace. Guard against empty self-satisfaction and pride. These have led many into error and into almost incurable blindness. Let the ruin of the proud and of those that are foolishly presumptuous be a warning to you. Let it keep you humble.

CHAPTER SEVEN

Grace Hidden under Humility

The Lord: Son, when you have the grace of devotion,

it is safer and more worthwhile to conceal it. Avoid being conceited about it. Do not talk a great deal about it. Do not think much about it. Despise yourself more and be fearful of this grace that is given to one who is unworthy. Do not become too ardently attached to this state. For it can easily change completely. When grace is with you, remember how unhappy and helpless you were without it. Progress in the spiritual life is not only experiencing the grace of comfort. It is also suffering the withdrawal of grace with meek humility. When grace is withdrawn, do not be slack in your prayers. Do not omit your other ordinary tasks. To the best of your ability and understanding be glad to do what you can. Do not neglect yourself when you experience dryness and anxiety of heart.

Many are quick to become impatient and slide back when they have no success. *The course of man is not in his control* (Jer 10: 23). It is for God to give comfort when, as much and to whom he pleases, just as much as he wishes and no more. Some unwise persons have worn themselves out because of the grace of comfort. They tried to do more than they could manage. They failed to understand the measure of their own smallness. They presumed to do more than God willed. So they lost grace quickly. They built their nests in heaven. Yet they became helpless mean castaways so that, humbled and impoverished, they might learn to trust in my wings and not fly off on their own. Novices are unskilled in the Lord's way. If they do not follow the advice of discreet persons, they can easily be deceived and slip.

When men wish to do what they like and do not trust others of proven experience, there will be a dangerous outcome; particularly if they are unwilling to give up their own opinions. Those who think themselves wise do not often accept the guidance of others. A little knowledge that is humble and not very clever is better than a great store of knowledge that is coupled with empty self-satisfaction. To have just a little is better than to have very much. Having very much can make you proud. A man who is always ready to have a good time does not behave very wisely. He forgets how weak he was in the beginning. He forgets that simple reverence which is fearful of losing the grace that was given. Whenever difficulty and opposition come, it is not very virtuous to become too despondent and trust in me less than you should.

A man who is too anxious for security in peacetime is found often to be too scared and frightened in time of war. If you know how to remain meek and think little of yourself, if you can guide and govern your own spirit, you will not easily meet danger or attack. When you are caught in rapture of spirit you are well advised to think what will happen when the light leaves you. But, when it does happen, remember that the light will come back. It was removed as a warning to you and for my glory.

A trial like this is often more helpful than that things should always go as well as you wish. A man's merits are not counted by the visions and comforts he experiences, by his skill in the Scriptures or by the high position in which he is placed. What is important is that he is truly grounded in humility, that he is filled with divine charity, that he has no great opinion of himself and that he prefers to be despised and put down by others rather than to be honoured.

80

CHAPTER EIGHT

Low Self-Esteem

*The Servant: I am bold to speak like this to my Lord,
I who am but dust and ashes* (Gen 18: 27). If I think
myself greater than this, then you stand against me.
My sins witness this. I cannot deny it. Let me belittle
myself. Let me think little of myself and cast off self-
esteem. In so far as I count myself as dust, your grace
will favour me and your light will be my heart's
companion. All self-esteem, no matter how little it is,
will be swallowed up in the pit of my nothingness
and will perish. In this pit you show to me myself,
what I am, what I was and what I have become. I
failed to understand that I am nothing (cf Ps 73: 21).
When I am left to myself, I am nothing, just weakness
itself. Yet, if for a moment you look at me, immediately
I am filled with gladness. The great wonder is the
suddenness with which I am uplifted, the tenderness
with which you embrace me. My own weight always
pulls me down.

It is your love that brings this about. It is my unpaid
guide. It supports me in my many needs. It saves me
from uncountable dangers. By loving myself badly I
lost myself. By yearning for you and simply loving
you, I found both you and myself. By that love I have
brought myself deeper into nothingness. You do with
me, my sweetest, more than I deserve, more than I
dare pray for or expect.

May you be blessed, my God. I am unfit for any
good. Yet, even when I am ungrateful and turn away
from you, your nobility and boundless goodness never

cease to benefit me. Bring us to you. Let us be thankful, humble and committed. You are our salvation, our power and our strength.

CHAPTER NINE

God, the End of All

The Lord: Son, if you wish true happiness, I must be your supreme and ultimate end. Thus your love can be cleansed. It is so often misdirected towards creatures and to yourself. Seeking yourself in anything soon makes you weak and dry. Refer everything to me above all. I am the giver of everything. See everything as linked with the sovereign good. It must be brought back to its source in me.

I am the living fountainhead. From me the weak and the strong, the poor and the rich draw life-giving water. Those who serve me willingly and gladly will receive *grace in return for grace* (Jn 1: 16). The man who seeks joy in any private possession or who aims for glory that is apart from me will not remain really happy. His heart will not be open. It will be restricted and restrained. You should claim no credit for any good that is in you. You should not say that any man is virtuous. Give everything to God. Without him man has nothing. I have given everything. I want everything returned to me. I am strict in demanding thanks.

Empty glory is put to flight by this truth. Where heavenly grace and real charity have entered there will be no envy. Narrowness of heart and self-love will have no place. Divine charity is all-conquering. It expands the soul's powers. Those of you who have proper understanding will rejoice and trust in me alone. *No one is good but God alone* (Lk 18: 19). He is to be praised above all things and blessed in all things.

CHAPTER TEN

The Sweet Service of God

The Servant: I shall speak once more, Lord, and I will not be silent. I will speak in the ears of my Lord, my God, my king who is on high: *Yahweh, how great is your goodness reserved for those who fear you* (Ps 31: 19). What are you to those who love you? What are you to those who serve you wholeheartedly? The sweetness of the contemplation you give to those who love you is really beyond words. The greatest way you show me your sweetness is that I was not and you made me. When I wandered far from you you brought me back to your service. You have told me to love you.

What shall I say to you, O Fount of eternal Love? How shall I forget you? You were willing to keep me in mind even when I was beaten and lost. You have been more kind to your servant than he ever dared expect. You have shown him more grace and friendship than he ever deserved. What shall I pay back for such grace? Not everybody is permitted to leave all, to renounce the world and enter the monastic life. Is it great that I should serve you in this way? Such service is the obligation of every creature. I ought not to feel that serving you is a great burden. What seems great and wonderful to me is that you agree to take such a poor and unworthy person and make him one of your beloved servants.

All I have to serve you with is yours. Indeed the contrary is true. You serve me more than I serve you. You have created heaven and earth for the service of man. They are always ready to do what you command. This is little enough. You have commanded even the angels to serve man. You have promised to give yourself to him.

What shall I give you in return for all these thousands of benefits? Would that I could serve you every day of my life! Would that I could serve you worthily even one day! You are worthy of all service, all glory and everlasting praise. You are my God and I am your poor servant. I should serve you with all my might. I should not expect any praise in return. That is my wish. That is my desire. Please, then, fill up what I lack.

To serve you and to despise everything else for your sake is great honour and glory. Those who give themselves willingly to your holy service possess great grace indeed. Those who cast aside all pleasure of the flesh for love of you will discover the Holy Spirit's sweetest comfort. Those who enter the narrow way in your name will achieve great freedom of mind. They will put aside all earthly worry.

O pleasant and delightful bondage to God, that makes man really free and holy! O holy state of religious service, that makes man like the angels, pleasing to God, the terror of devils, an example to the faithful! O bondage that always must be embraced and ever must be accepted freely! It earns the supreme reward and receives endless lasting gladness.

CHAPTER ELEVEN

Control of the Heart's Desires

The Lord: Son, you have many things to learn. You have not yet learned them well.

The Servant: What are these things, Lord?

The Lord: You must put all your desires entirely under my control. You must not be a lover of self. You must hanker after my will. Desires often excite you and affect you strongly. Find out whether you are motivated by my glory or by your own convenience. If I am the source, you will be satisfied with whatever I arrange. Any hidden self-seeking that is present will hold you back and weigh you down.

Take care, therefore, for fear you make too much of any desire that is conceived without consulting me. What pleased you at first and you worked hard for as the better thing might become unpleasant. Do not go straight after every desire that seems good. Do not simply avoid every desire that is awkward. It is right to use restraint even in good intentions and desires. If indulged in at the wrong time, they might give bad example to others. If others oppose them, you might soon become upset and give up.

Sometimes you must use violence and put up strong resistance to the desires of your senses. Pay no heed to what the flesh wants or does not want. Work hard to bring about even its unwilling subjection to the spirit. It should be chastised and forced under control until it is fully prepared to be satisfied with little, to take pleasure in little things and not to grumble about discomfort.

CHAPTER TWELVE

Patient Resistance to Lust

The Servant: It seems to me, Lord, that I have great need of patience. Much of what happens in this life is upsetting. No matter what I do to be at peace, my life cannot be without strife and grief.

The Lord: Son, that is true. But I do not want you to seek such peace as is without trial and feels no opposition. Realise, however, that you have found peace, even at those times when suffering tries you and opposition tests you.

You say perhaps that you cannot suffer much. How then will you put up with the fires of purgatory? You must always choose the lesser of two evils. In order to escape the everlasting punishments of the future you should choose calmly to undergo the ills of the present. Do you think that men of the world suffer little or nothing? You may ask even even those who live in the greatest luxury. You will find that it is not so.

The Servant: But they have many luxuries and do what they like. Therefore they make light of their sufferings.

The Lord: They may have all they want. But how long do you think it will last? Those who are rich in the world's goods *will vanish like smoke* (Ps 37: 20). Past pleasures will not even be remembered. To enjoy these pleasures even in this life involves bitterness, boredom and fear. The very things that give them delight have within them the source of their pitiful punishment. It is right that those who rush madly after luxuries should not enjoy them without shame and bitterness.

How short and sham, how rank and rotten they all are! Yet, besotted and blind, they fail to understand. Like dumb animals, they permit the death of the soul for the sake of a little pleasure in this corruptible life. But you, my son, *Do not follow your lusts, restrain your desires* (Sir 18: 30). *Make Yahweh your only joy and he will give you what your heart desires* (Ps 37: 4).

If it is your wish to have real pleasure and fuller comfort in me, you will be happy to condemn all worldly things and to cut yourself off from all weak pleasures. You will be given plenty of comfort. The more you give up all pleasure in created things, the sweeter and greater comfort you will find in me. In the beginning, however, you will not reach this comfort without some sadness and some struggling effort. Ingrained habit will hinder you, but will be overcome by better habit. The flesh will complain, but will be reined in by the ardour of the spirit. The old serpent will goad and annoy you, but prayer will put him to flight. Furthermore, hard work will help to block his easy approach to you.

CHAPTER THIRTEEN

Obedience modelled on Jesus Christ

The Lord: Son, to seek to be rid of obedience is to be rid of grace. To work hard for personal profit is to lose goods that are common. A man who is not willing to obey shows that his flesh is not yet under complete control. It often grumbles and is stubborn. Learn quick submission to your superior if you want control over your own flesh. If the inward man is not defeated, the enemy will be overcome more quickly. When you are not one with the spirit, the soul has no worse or no more troublesome enemy than yourself. If you wish to overcome flesh and blood, you should always have a low opinion of yourself. Your love of self is as yet too undisciplined. You are afraid, therefore, to place yourself completely under the direction of others.

Is it such a great thing that for God's sake you should submit to others? Are you not dust and nothing? Have I, the almighty and most high, not submitted myself to man for your sake? I became the least and the humblest of all that by my humility I might conquer your pride. Dust that you are, learn to obey. Muck and earth that you are, learn to be humble and to bow down at the feet of everyone. Learn to control your will and to submit to everyone. Flare up at yourself and do not allow yourself to swell with pride. Show yourself submissive and to be of little importance. Let everyone walk over you and trample you like street refuse. What have you to complain of, vain man? Are you not a dirty sinner? Have you not offended God often, and more often deserved hell? I have looked on you mercifully because I regard you as precious. I wish you to understand my love and to be grateful always for the blessings I give you. I wish you always to submit yourself to real obedience and humility. I wish you to be long suffering when you are despised.

CHAPTER FOURTEEN

God's Judgement and our Pride

The Servant: Lord, you pronounce your judgements over me. Fear and trembling shake my whole frame. My soul quakes very much. I am astonished when I consider *the heavens are not in your eyes clean. If you even found fault with the angels* (cf Job 15: 15; 4: 18) and did not forgive them, what is to happen to me? *The stars of the sky fell* (Rev 6: 13 and Is 34: 4). What dare I do? I am only dust. Those whose actions seemed worth praising have fallen right down. I have seen those who ate the bread of angels take pleasure in the husks of swine.

If you, Lord, withdraw the support of your hand, no holiness can exist. If you do not guide, there is no help in wisdom. If you do not guard, no chastity is safe. Without your holy watchfulness no guard over ourselves is effective. If you leave us, we sink and die. If you visit us, we get up and live. Alone, we are unstable; but through you we are strengthened. We are cool; but through you we are set on fire.

Should I not look upon myself as a humble reject? When I seem to have something good, should I not value it as nothing? Should I not bend down deeply in the face of your unquestionable judgements? Lord, where can I find anything in myself that is other than nothing, only nothing? O immeasurable weight! O uncrossable sea, where I find myself nothing, altogether nothing! Where is glory's den? Where is trust and virtue conceived? All empty boasting is swallowed up in the depths of your judgements upon me.

What do you think of all flesh? Is the clay better than the potter? (cf Is 29: 18). If a man's heart is really submissive to God, how can empty chatter make him proud? If a man submits himself to the truth, the whole world cannot make him proud. If he has placed all his trust in God, he will be unaffected by the words of all those that praise him. Indeed all those who speak are themselves nothing. When the sound of their words goes they go too. *Yahweh's faithfulness is eternal* (Ps 117: 2).

CHAPTER FIFTEEN

Doing the Will of God

The Lord: Son, always say: Lord, let what pleases you be done. Lord, let what honours you be done in your name. Lord, if you judge anything to be for my good and regard it as useful for me, then let me use that gift for your glory. If, however, you know that any wish of mine is harmful and of no value for the salvation of my soul, take such a wish away from me. Not every wish that men regard as right and proper comes from the Holy Spirit. It is difficult to discern whether the spirit that moves you to desire this or that is good or not. You may be motivated even by your own spirit. Many who seemed at first to have been led by a good spirit have been deceived in the end.

Whatever, therefore, is perceived as desirable should always be begged for with a God-fearing humble heart. Have a deep distrust of self. Leave everything to me. Affirm: Lord you know what is best. Let whatever you wish be done. Give what you wish, as much as you wish and whenever you wish. Deal with me as you know how and as you please. Let whatever is done for me be for your greater glory. Put me wherever you wish and be free in all you do with me. I am in your hands, to be swung around and about. I am your servant, ready for anything. I want to live, not for myself, but for you. Would that I were completely worthy.

PRAYER: Tenderest Jesus, grant me your grace. Let it be with me. Let it work with me. Let it stay with me until the end. Make me always wish and desire whatever you find most acceptable and most lovingly pleasant. Let your will be mine and my will always imitate and match yours. Let my liking and disliking be the same as yours. Make my wishing follow what you wish. Let me avoid what you do not wish. Make me dead to all worldly things. Make me desire to be despised and unknown for your sake. Above all make me desire to find rest in you and find peace of heart in you. You are the heart's real peace, its only rest. Everything outside you is hard and irritating. *In peace*, that is, in the everlasting good, *I lie down and fall asleep at once* (Ps 4: 9). Amen.

CHAPTER SIXTEEN

Seek Real Comfort in God

Whatever personal comfort I can desire and imagine I hope for hereafter and not here. If I alone could have all the world's comforts and enjoy all its luxuries, it would certainly not last long. Therefore, my soul, you cannot be completely comforted nor perfectly happy except in God, the comforter of the poor and the support of the humble. Tarry a while, my soul. Wait on God's promise. In heaven you will have plenty of all that is good. If you are too undisciplined in your desire for the things of the present, you will lose those that are everlasting. Use what is temporal. Yearn for what is eternal. No temporal good can satisfy you. You were not made to enjoy such things.

Even if you possessed all temporal goods, you could not be blissfully happy. All blissfulness and all happiness is in God, the creator of everything. This is not what the world's lovers see and praise. It is that for which good faithful christians yearn. Sometimes persons who are spiritual and pure of heart have a foretaste of it. Their whole conversation concerns heavenly things. All human comfort is short-lived and empty. That comfort which is grasped inwardly by the truth is real and happy. The committed person carries Jesus, his comforter, with him everywhere. Let my comfort be that I will gladly miss all human comfort. When your comfort is absent, let your will and the test it is your right to apply be my greatest comfort. *His indignation does not last for ever, his resentment exists for a short time only* (Ps 103: 9).

CHAPTER SEVENTEEN

Put everything in God's Care

The Lord: Son, let me do what I want with you. I know what is best for you. You think as a man. In many things your feelings are guided by human appetites.

The Servant: What you say is true, Lord. Your care for me is greater than any care I can have for myself. He who does not place everything in your care puts himself in a very unhappy position. Lord, do what you will with me. Only let my will stay right and steady. Whatever you do with me can only be good. You may wish me to be in darkness. May you be blessed. You may wish me to be in light. May you again be blessed. You may wish me to be comforted. May you be blessed. You may wish me to suffer sorrow. May you be equally blessed.

The Lord: Son, if you wish to walk with me, this is what you must do. You should be as ready to suffer as to rejoice. You must gladly accept want and poverty as well as plenty and riches.

The Servant: For you I will suffer gladly, Lord, whatever you wish to happen to me. From your hand I will accept with indifference the good and the ill, the sweet and the bitter, the joyful and the sad. I wish to be thankful for all that happens to me. Guard me from sin and I will fear neither death nor hell. Do not ever cast me out. Do not blot my name out from the book of life. No trial that comes to me can harm me.

CHAPTER EIGHTEEN

Christ, the Model of Patient Suffering

The Lord: Son, I came down from heaven to save you. Moved by love, not by any need, I took on your sorrow to teach you to bear this passing sadness with patient courage. From the moment of my birth until I passed away on the cross I did not lack sorrows to suffer. I was in great want of the goods of this world. People often complained about me. I bore shame and reproach with meekness. I got ingratitude for my good deeds. I was cursed for my miracles and rebuked for my teaching.

The Servant: Lord, by suffering in this life you fulfilled your Father's command completely. It is right then that, following your will, a miserable sinner like me should suffer with patience. So long as you will it I should carry the burden of this corruptible life to gain salvation. I feel the burden of this life. Yet your grace makes it full of merit. By following your example, in the footsteps of the saints, the weak find life more glorious and more bearable. Indeed we have much more comfort now than was given under the old law. Then heaven's gate was firmly shut. Even the way to heaven seemed dark. Few cared to seek the kingdom of heaven. Even those who were so justified as to be saved could not enter the heavenly kingdom until you had suffered and made atonement by your holy death.

What great thanks I should give to you for showing me and all the faithful the right way to your eternal kingdom! Your life is our way. We come to you through holy patience. You are our crown. If you had not gone ahead and shown the way, who would have bothered to follow? How many would have stayed far behind if they had not seen your shining example? We have heard of your teaching and your wonders. Yet we are still lukewarm. What would happen to us if we did not have your great light to follow?

CHAPTER NINETEEN

The Genuinely Patient Man

The Lord: Son, what are you saying? Cease complaining. Think of my sufferings and the sufferings of the saints. *You have not yet had to keep fighting to the point of death* (Heb 12: 4). Your suffering is little, compared with the many sufferings others have endured. They were sorely tempted, severely tried, tested and proved in many ways. You should call to mind the grievous sufferings of others. Then you would make light of the little ones you suffer. Maybe they do not seem very little to you. Make sure that you do not think this on account of your impatience. Whether your sufferings be little or big, try hard to bear them patiently.

In so far as you make up your mind to be more patient you act more wisely and earn a fuller reward. If you strive hard to achieve an attitude and habit of acceptance, your sufferings will be borne more easily. Do not say: I cannot take this from that man. I ought not to have to suffer such things. He has done me harm. He has accused me of things that never entered my mind. Yet I will put up with it from another man.

I will see it as something I ought to suffer. Such an idea is foolish. It pays heed neither to the virtue of patience nor to him who will reward it. It tallies persons and the wrongs you suffer.

A man who will suffer only what he understands or from people that he likes is not really patient. A really patient man pays no heed to who bothers him, whether he is his superior, his equal or his subject, a good holy man or an awkward unworthy person. From every creature alike, he accepts as from God's hand whatever comes to him, no matter how great it is or how often it comes. He considers this a great gain. There is nothing so little that it does not have some merit in God's eyes. It must, however, be suffered for his sake.

Be ready to fight, therefore, if you wish victory. You will not gain the crown of patience without a fight. If you do not wish to suffer, you refuse the crown. If you wish to be crowned, be manful and suffer patiently. Rest is always preceded by work. Fighting always comes before victory.

The Servant: Lord, grace makes me able to do what seemed naturally impossible. You know how little I can suffer, how quickly I give up in the face of even a little difficulty. Lord, let any kind of trial become pleasant and desirable to me. Suffering and affliction for your sake is good for my soul.

CHAPTER TWENTY

Admitting Weakness

The Servant: I will confess my fault (Ps 32: 6). I will

admit my weakness to you, my Lord. I am often upset and downcast by small things. I think myself safe whenever I do not experience temptation. Then I find myself almost bowled over by a little puff of wind.

Take note, therefore, Lord, of my humility and weakness. You know them well. Have mercy on me. *Pull me out of this swamp; let me sink no further* (Ps 69: 14). Let me not ever be cast down. This is what beats me back and fills me with confusion in your presence. I am so ready to slip and so weak in resisting lust. Even though I do not consent entirely, the assault of lust is still a bother and a burden to me. The daily strife of living wearies me. I know my weakness. Awful imaginings rush in on me always more readily than they go.

Most mighty God of Israel, zealous lover of faithful souls, consider graciously the toil and sorrow of your servant. Stand by him always, wherever he goes. Stiffen me with heavenly strength. Do not let the old man, my wretched flesh, still incompletely subject to the spirit, gain the upper hand. It is against this I should strive so long as I have breath in this miserable life. The enemy's traps are all around. When one trial or temptation goes, another takes its place, even while we are still fighting the previous temptation. When we least expect them, many more come upon us. How can we love a life so full of bitterness, so filled with sorrow and calamity? How can it be called life at all when it begets so many deaths and diseases? And yet it is loved and many seek to enjoy it. The world is often condemned as false and empty. Yet the flesh's desires are so strong in us that it is not easy to give it up. Some things make us love the world, others make us hate it. We are attracted to the world by the flesh's desires, the curiosity of the eyes and by the pride of life. But the just punishments that follow these bring about weariness and hatred of the world.

Alas! Delight in evil controls a mind that is dedicated to the world and finds its thorny entanglements pleasant. Such a mind has neither seen nor sensed God's sweetness nor the inward pleasantness of virtue. Let men despise the world perfectly and strive under the holy rule to live for God. They will not be ignorant of the sweetness God has promised those who give up the world. They understand clearly and distinctly that the world is grievously mistaken and deceived.

CHAPTER TWENTY ONE

God, the Source of All Good

The Servant: God is the everlasting resting place of all the saints. You should, therefore, my soul, seek your rest only in the Lord, not in any other good. Most sweet and loving Jesus, let me rest in you alone. Let me put little value on any created thing: health and beauty, glory and honour, power and dignity, knowledge and finesse, riches and treasures, pleasure and gladness, fame and renown, sweetness and consolation, hope and expectation, merit and yearning, gifts and presents, all that you can give and endow, glee and jubilation, all the mind can grasp and feel, even the angels and archangels, everything that is not you, my God.

You, my Lord God, are the best. You are the highest.

You are the most powerful, the fullest and the most self-sufficient. You are the most sweet and comforting, the most beautiful and lovable, the noblest and most praiseworthy of all. Every good quality is at once perfect in you. It has always been so. It will always be so. Whatever you give me besides yourself is small and incomplete. Whatever you reveal and promise about yourself I cannot grasp fully until I come face to face with you. My heart can neither be fully at rest nor properly contented until it reaches beyond all gifts and creatures and rests in you.

Jesus Christ, my dearest spouse, most pure lover and ruler of all creation, *How far could I take my flight* (Ps 55: 7) to be free and stay with you? When may I see and experience fully how kind you are, my Lord God? When can I be so closely joined with you as to lose all sense of self? When may I embrace you in a way that is beyond feeling and measure, beyond common knowledge? Now I sigh often and suffer sorrowful unhappiness. In this valley of sorrows, there are many evils. They upset me. They make me sad. They cloud my happiness. They block my way. They distract me. They pull me and entangle me so that I cannot approach you openly and enjoy the pleasure of those embraces that you give to spirits that are blessed. May my sighs and the many sorrows I suffer here move you.

O Jesus, brightness of everlasting glory, balm of the pilgrim soul, my lips are wordless in your presence. My silence speaks to you. Why does my Lord delay? Let him come to poor little me and make me glad. Let him put out his hand and lift me from my misery and anxiety. Come; come; you are my delight. Without you, no day, no hour is pleasant. Without you, my table is bare. I am as sad as a man imprisoned, weighed down with shackles, when I am not refreshed with the light of your presence, when you deny me freedom or even a friendly glance.

Let others go after what they like. Nothing except you can please me. You are my God, my hope, my everlasting safety. I will not be silent. I will continue to plead for the return of your grace. I will beg you to speak to me inwardly.

The Lord: *I am here* (Is 58: 9). I have come because you asked me. Your tears, your soul's yearning and your humble sorrow have persuaded me to come to you.

The Servant: I said: Lord, I have called you. I wanted to enjoy you. I was ready to give up everything for you. It was you, however, who first moved me to seek you. *You have been good to your servant* (Ps 119: 65). You are very merciful. What can your servant say? He can remember only his meanness and his sin. He can humble himself, simply humble himself before you. Of all the wonders of heaven and earth nothing equals you. Your deeds are good. Your judgements are true. Your foresight supports the universe. To you be praise and honour, Wisdom of the Father. May my mouth and my soul be one with all creation in praising and blessing you.

CHAPTER TWENTY TWO

Remember God's Many Blessings

The Servant: Lord, make me welcome your law. Teach

me to follow your commands. Let me know your will.
Let me keep carefully before my mind a very reverent
awareness of all the good you do for me, the ordinary
as well as the extraordinary things. In this way I may
manage to thank you properly. I know well and admit
that I cannot give you even the least part of the praise
and thanks you deserve. I am less than all the good
things that you give me. My spirit falters before the
greatness of the nobility I recognise in you.

You have given us all our spiritual and bodily
possessions, whether outward or inward, natural or
supernatural, all the things we own. These gifts show
that you are generous, loving and good. We receive
from you all that is good. Some have more. Some have
less. Yet, all is yours. Even the smallest thing cannot
be owned without your willing it.

When a man has more, he has no right to be proud,
to boast or to scorn the man who has less. The better
man and the greater man is the man who thinks he
is the least, the man who gives thanks with greater
modesty and devotion. A man who regards himself as
meaner than all and judges himself to be less worthy
is more fit to receive greater gifts.

The man who has less ought not to be sad, take it
amiss or envy the man who is richer. He should look
to you and praise your goodness. For you have given
your gifts generously, freely, gladly and without
favouritism. Everything comes from you. You must
be praised in everything. You know what should be
given to each. You know why this man should have
less and the other more. It is not we who decide these
things, but you. For you are able to judge the merits
of each case.

Therefore, Lord God, I think it is a blessing that I do not have many of the things that men think worth praise and honour. A man who sees that he is poor and mean should not be heavy-hearted, sad or dispirited. He should be comforted and be glad. For you, God, chose for your close friends and servants the poor, the humble and those the world despised. Your apostles are your witnesses. You made them princes over all the earth (cf Ps 44: 17). As far as the world was concerned, they were faultless (cf Phil 3: 6). With simple humility, innocent of malice or of guile, they were glad to be scorned in your name (cf Ac 6: 41). They embraced affectionately the things the world despised.

The man who loves you and knows your blessings should rejoice in nothing so much as your will for him, no matter what your eternal providence is pleased to arrange. He should be content and happy with this. He should be just as happy to be the least as others are who choose to be the greatest. He should be as meek and contented when he is placed last as when he is placed first. He should be as glad to be humbled and scorned, to lack reputation and good name, as to be praised by others and placed high in the world. Your will and the desire for your glory should be more important than anything. They should give him more comfort and please him more than any blessings he has received or will receive.

CHAPTER TWENTY THREE

The Four Founts of Peace

The Lord: Son, I will now show the way to peace and real freedom.

The Servant: Do as you say, Lord. I am ready to listen.

The Lord: Son, strive to do the will of others rather than your own.

Prefer always to have less than to have more.

Seek the lower place beneath all others.

Choose and pray that God's will may be fully realised in you.

A man who does this crosses the borders of peace and rest.

The Servant: Lord, this short lesson holds much perfection. Few words indeed, but replete with meaning and full of fruit. If I could keep them faithfully I would not be upset so easily. Whenever I feel bad or heavy-hearted, I recognise that I have ignored this lesson. You can do everything. You wish the soul to become perfect. Fill me with greater grace so that I may live this lesson fully and be perfectly saved.

Lord, my God, *Do not stand aside, my God, come quickly and help me* (Ps 71: 12). Great fears and many worries surge up in me. They afflict my soul. How can I endure them and come to no harm? How can I break them? *I will go before you*, he says, *levelling the heights* (Is 45: 2). I will open the prison gates and show you the hidden secrets. Do what you say, Lord, and put all evil thoughts to flight. My only hope of consolation is to run to you in time of trouble, to trust you, to pray to you from the bottom of my heart and to wait patiently for your comfort.

Good Jesus, enlighten me with brilliant inward light. Cast out all darkness from the haven of my heart. Bring my wandering thoughts under control. Destroy the temptations that have such power over me. Be strong in battle for me. Expel the wild beast, namely, the lusts that tantalise me. May *peace* be *inside your city walls* (Ps 122: 7) and praise resound in the holy hall, that is, in the clear conscience. Command the winds and the storms. Say to the sea: 'Be still' and to the north wind: 'Do not blow'. *Send out your light and your truth* (Ps 43: 3) to shine over the earth. I am earth, I am empty, I am void unless you enlighten me. Pour down your grace. Bathe my heart in heavenly dew. Bring waters of devotion to water the face of the earth and make it fully fruitful. My mind is weighed down with the great stone that is my sins. Lift it up. Hang all my hopes on heaven. If I taste the sweetness of eternal happiness, I will be slow to think of earthly things. Grasp me and rescue me from passing creature comforts. Let no desire for created things satisfy me or content me fully. Join me to you with an unbreakable link of love. You alone can satisfy the lover. Apart from you, everything is unimportant.

CHAPTER TWENTY FOUR

Avoid Curiosity about the Lives of Others

The Lord: Son, do not be inquisitive. Do not busy yourself with idle cares. What does this or that matter *to you? You are to follow me* (Jn 21: 22). What does it matter to you that one man is such and such or another does this or says that? You do not have to answer for others. It is yourself that you have to justify. Why get involved? I know and see everything under the sun. I know what each man is like, what he thinks, what he wants and what his aims are. I have everything under control. Look after yourself. Leave the agitator to agitate as much as he likes. Whatever he does or says will come back to him. He cannot cheat me.

Pay no heed to the shadow of a great name. Do not seek friendship with many or the particular affection of any man. For these beget distraction and cloud the heart. Be glad to repeat my word to yourself and I will reveal what is hidden, so long as you take careful note of my coming and open your heart to me. Be ready. Watch and pray. Be humble in everything.

CHAPTER TWENTY FIVE

True Peace and Real Progress

The Lord: Son, I have said: *Peace I bequeath to you, my own peace I give you, a peace the world cannot give, this is my gift to you* (Jn 14: 27). Everybody wants peace; but not everybody cares about what really brings peace. The meek and gentle have my peace. If you are to be at peace, you must be patient. If you listen to me and do what I say, you can enjoy great peace.

The Servant: What should I do, then?

The Lord: Always be careful. Watch what you do. Watch what you say. In everything, go after this aim. Try to please me. Do not desire or seek anything beyond me. Avoid rash judgement concerning what others do or say. Do not meddle in matters that do not concern you. In this way you can hardly ever be troubled.

This is not the life when you will neither feel trouble nor suffer illness of body or soul. Such is the state of eternal rest. When you feel no burden, do not think that you have found real peace. When you have no one against you, do not judge that all is well. When everything goes the way you like it, do not believe that all is right. If you experience great devotion and pleasure, do not, therefore, think that you are of special worth or are particularly loved. These are not marks by which the true lover is recognised. Nor are they the signs of a man's progress in perfection.

The Servant: What, therefore, is perfection, Lord?

The Lord: You must submit yourself fully to the will of God. Do not be selfish (cf 1 Cor 13: 5) in matters small or great, in matters of time or eternity. In this way you may be equally grateful for everything. You will measure both prosperity and adversity by the same yardstick. If you become so strong and so long-suffering that you can lose all inward comfort and still be ready to suffer more, if you do not complain that you have to suffer so much, if you accept whatever I arrange and praise it, then you are walking along the right road to peace. You can have certain hope that you will rejoice sometime in my presence. If you have reached complete self-contempt, you can be sure that

you will enjoy great peace, as much as you can cope
with here on earth.

CHAPTER TWENTY SIX

Prayer and Mental Freedom

The Servant: Lord, the perfect man ought never to
take his mind off heavenly things. Though full of
cares, he should go along as if he had not a worry in
the world, not because he is too lazy to bother, but
because he has the gift of mental freedom. This gift
stops him clinging to undisciplined love of creatures.

Most loving God, I beg you to keep me free from
too great concern for the cares of this life. Keep me
free of the body's needs for fear I give in to luxury.
Keep my mind clear in case, broken by troubles, I
falter. I speak not only of the vanities of the world
that surround us all, but also of those ills that are the
common curse of mortals. For they hold your servant
back. No matter how often he wishes it, he cannot
achieve spiritual freedom.

O God of indescribable sweetness, make all bodily
comfort bitter to me. For it pulls me away from
everlasting love. It dangles wickedly before me the
desire for pleasure here and now. Let me win, Lord.
Let me not be beaten by flesh and blood. Let me not
be deceived by the passing glory of the world. Let me
not be tripped by the devil's wiles. Give me the power
to resist, the patience to suffer and the strength to
stand firm. In place of the world's comforts give me

the sweet unction of your spirit. In place of the love of the flesh fill me with the love of your name.

To the fervent spirit, food, drink, clothing and all that supports the body's needs are a burden. Let me be reasonable in using these things. Do not let me get too involved with them. To ignore them completely is not right. For life must be preserved. But the law of holiness forbids us to demand more than we need or to seek after those things which simply bring pleasure. To behave in this way might make the body rebel against the spirit. I pray you, let your hand lead me so that I do not have too many of these comforts.

CHAPTER TWENTY SEVEN

The Hindrance of Self-Love

The Lord: Son, to gain all you should give all. You should keep nothing to yourself. Self love certainly does you more harm than anything else in the world. The love and affection you have for anything is the measure of your attachment to it. If your love is pure, simple and well disciplined, you will be a slave to nothing. Do not yearn for what you may not have. Own nothing that can hinder or rob you of your inward freedom. The wonder is that you do not entrust yourself with all that you can own and desire totally to me.

Why are you eaten up with useless worry? Why do you exhaust yourself with needless concerns? You will come to no harm if you let me do as I please with you. You may seek this or that. You may go after convenience and pleasure either here or there. Yet you can never be quite free from care. You will never find anything that is perfect nor any place without someone to oppose you.

Getting possessions and increasing them is not what helps you. Condemning possessions and rooting them out of yourself are what give you benefit. This holds good not only for money and riches, but also for ambition and the desire for empty praise. These all end when the world ends. To stay where you are is not much defence, if you are discontented. The peace you seek elsewhere will not last, so long as your heart lacks a true anchor. If you do not stand by me, you can certainly change. But you will not improve. The result will be that you rediscover the very things from which you ran away, and more besides.

PRAYER: Give me power through your spirit, God, that my hidden self may grow strong. Empty my heart of all useless worry and anxiety. Do not let me be drawn by any desire for mean or for precious things. Let me realise that all things pass away and that with them I too will pass away. There is nothing permanent under the sun. How empty it is! How spiritually bothersome! The man who thinks in this way is wise indeed.

Lord, grant me heavenly wisdom. Teach me to be steady in my search for you alone. Let me relish and love you more than anything. Let me understand all other things the way they are, that is, the way you planned them. Make me avoid the flatterer and suffer the critic. It is indeed great wisdom not to winnow in every wind and to ignore the scandalous talk of the siren. The road on which we start will be the one we travel.

CHAPTER TWENTY EIGHT

Slander

The Lord: Son, do not get upset if people have a low opinion of you or say about you what you would rather not hear. You should have an even lower opinion of yourself. You should not think of anyone as weaker than yourself. If you are an inward person, you will not bother much about wagging tongues. It is very prudent indeed to be silent when times are bad, not to be disturbed by men's opinion of you and to turn to me inwardly.

Do not expect peace from what men say of you. They might say that you are good or that you are bad. You will not become a changed man because of that. Where can one find real peace and true honour? Where else but in me? A man who neither desires to please men nor is afraid of antagonising them enjoys great peace. The heart's every distress and the mind's every distraction arise from undisciplined love and baseless fear.

CHAPTER TWENTY NINE

Bless God When Times are Hard

The Servant: May your name be blessed for ever, Lord

(Tob 3: 11). You willed that I should have this trial and sorrow. I cannot fly away from it. So, I need to fly to you. You can help me and make it good for me. Now I am sorrowful, Lord. I am ill at ease. I am upset by the present suffering. What can I say now, Lord? I am pressed in on all sides. *Father, save me from this hour.*

But it was for this reason that I came to this hour (Jn 12: 27, 28) that you might be honoured. For I am really humbled. By you I have been freed. *O come and rescue me, Lord* (Ps 40: 13). I am poor. What can I do? Where can I go without you? Give me patience, Lord, even now. Help me, my God. I will not be afraid, no matter what sorrow is given me to bear.

What can I say now? *Lord, may your will be done* (Mt 6: 10). I have deserved to be put on trial and to be weighed down. I just have to bear it. I have to hold on until the storm is over and things get better. Your almighty hand is powerful. It can lift away this temptation and weaken its impact so that I do not give in to it. My God and my mercy, you have often done this for me before. The more difficult it is for me, the easier it is for you 'to change the right hand of the most high'* (Ps 77: 10).

---

*The typical edition of the Vulgate gives three variant readings for this text. The German and Spanish translations consulted follow the reading used here. The Italian and Jerusalem do not follow this reading. It is difficult to know exactly what the text means here. So it is left as the *Imitatio* has it.

CHAPTER THIRTY

Confidence in God's Help

The Lord: Son, I am the Lord, *a stronghold in the day of distress* (Nah 1: 7). When things go badly for you you can come to me. Your greatest obstacle to heavenly joy is that you leave it to the last moment before you turn to me in prayer. Before you turn to me with your earnest petition you seek first your consolation and refreshment in outward things. That is why you achieve little success. You must realise that I am the one who saves those who trust in me. The aid that is outside me is ineffective. Outside me there is no advice that is not useless, no remedy that is lasting. Now that the tempest is over and you have got your breath back, you can regain your strength by considering my mercy. I am ready (the Lord says) to restore everything, not just the way it was, but a good deal more besides.

Is anything difficult for me? Am I a person who talks and does not do?

Where is your trust? Be firm and stubborn, long-suffering and strong. At the right time, happiness will come to you. Wait! Wait for me. I will come and heal you. You are vexed with temptation. Empty fear scares you. What can worry about what the future may bring do for you? Can it bring you anything other than one sorrow piled upon another? *Each day has enough trouble of its own* (Mt 6: 34). It is pointless and useless to worry or be gratified about what might be. It may not come off at all.

It is but human to be teased by such imaginings. It is a sign of a weak spirit to be easily influenced by the

suggestions of the enemy. He does not care whether
he uses truth or falsehood to delude and deceive you.
He will knock you down just as much by your love
of the present as by your fear of the future. Do not,
therefore, become upset or afraid. Trust in me. Have
faith in my mercy. When you think yourself far from
me I am actually quite near. When you think you are
almost lost, great gain and merit are often at hand.
When things go against you, all is not lost. You should
not judge by present appearances. Do not succumb to
anything wearisome, no matter what its source, as
though you had lost all hope of handling it.

Do not think you have been completely deserted
when, for a time, I withdraw my consolation or send
you some trial. Such is the way to heaven. It is indeed
better for you as well as for my other servants that
you should not have everything the way you like. I
know those thoughts that are hidden. It is better for
your safety that sometimes you lack satisfaction. For
success can make you take conceited delight in what
you are not. What I have given I can take away. I can
give it back too when I am ready.

What I give is still mine. When I take it away I do
not take what is yours. Every good given is still mine,
All that is good, all that is perfect (Jas 1: 17). When I
send you sorrow and adversity, do not become indignant. Do not be down hearted. For I can quickly lift
you up again so that every burden becomes a joy.
Whenever I treat you in this way, I am just. You
should praise me very much.

If you have the right attitude and proper viewpoint,
you ought not to become sad and dejected. You should
rather give thanks and praise. Even when I do not

spare you and send you sorrow, you should consider it a reason for joy. *As the Father has loved me so I have loved you* (Jn 15: 9). This is what I said to my disciples. I did not send them great earthly joys. I sent them strife. I sent them not honours, but contempt, not idleness, just work, not rest, but the patience to be fruitful. Keep these words in mind, my son.

CHAPTER THIRTY ONE

Ignore Creatures to Find the Creator

The Servant: Lord, if I am to reach the stage where neither man nor creature can hinder me, I am in need of even greater grace. While I am held down by anything at all, I cannot be free to fly to you. The man who once said: *O for the wings of a dove to fly away and find rest* (Ps 55: 6), wished such free flight. Is there anything more at rest than the eye that is sound? Is there anyone on earth more free than the man who desires nothing? A man should rise above all that is created. He should get away from himself. Entranced, he should realise that you, the creator of all, have no created thing that is your equal. If a man is dependent on creatures, he cannot be free to go after what is divine. That is the reason why there are so few real contemplatives. Few people know how to cut themselves off from perishable created things.

This requires that great grace which lifts the soul up and holds it above itself. If a man is not lifted up in spirit, free from dependence on creatures and completely united to God, whatever he knows or possesses is of little value. The man who values greatly anything

besides the one immense, eternal good, will stay small.
He will stay on the ground for a long time. Whatever
is not God is nothing. It is to be valued as nothing.
What a difference there is between the wisdom of the
enlightened, committed man and the knowledge of
studiously learned clerks. The teaching that is infused
from above by God's influence is more noble than that
acquired by laborious human effort.

Many desire contemplation. Few want to make the
efforts necessary to achieve it. Their great weakness
is that they depend on visible signs and feelings. They
do not worry sufficiently about being fully dead to
self. I do not know what it is, by what spirit we are
guided or even what we reach out to when we seem
to be called spiritual. We make so much effort and
care so much about things that are mean and do not
last. It is very rarely that we gather our wits together
to think about what is inside us.

Alas! When we achieve a little recollection we are
too quick to go out. We do not make careful scrutiny
of what we do. We do not care if our desires sink low.
We do not become upset by all the impurity around
us. *For corrupt were the ways of all flesh* (Gen 6: 12).
This was the reason for the flood. Since, therefore, our
inward desire is so corrupt, the deed that results from
it is indeed also corrupt. For such a deed is but an
index of our lack of strength. The benefit of a good
life comes from a pure heart.

We ask how much a man has done. We inquire
seldom about the virtue that prompted his deeds. We
want to know if he is strong, rich, handsome, pleasant,
a good writer, a good singer or a good worker. Nobody
wants to know if he is poor in spirit, patient, meek,

committed or inward. Nature looks at the outside of a man. Grace looks at what is inward. Nature is often mistaken. Grace trusts in God in order to avoid error.

CHAPTER THIRTY TWO

Deny Yourself and Give up Greed

The Lord: Son, to be able to possess perfect freedom you must renounce yourself totally. Those who have property are shackled. So also are those who love themselves, the greedy, the inquisitive, the gadabouts and those who seek the things that are comfortable more than the things that are of Christ. Such people are for ever imagining and planning things that will not last. Everything that does not spring from God will perish. Keep before your mind this short, but perfect command: Renounce everything and you will gain everything. Give up greed and you will discover happiness. When you manage to get this into your head you will have perfect understanding.

The Servant: Lord, this is not the task of one day, no mere child's play. It is indeed a short summary of all religious perfection.

The Lord: Son, you have heard about the way of perfection. You should not be put off or upset by it. It should spur you on to higher things. At the least, it should fill you with a yearning desire for these things. It would be good if you were such a person and had reached such a stage that you are not a lover of self, but dependent simply on my will and the will of him whom I have placed over you as a father. Then you would please me very much. Your whole life would be spent in joy and peace. There is a great deal that you have still to renounce. To achieve what you desire you must place yourself totally in my hands. *Buy from me the gold that has been tested in the fire to make you really rich* (Rev 3: 18). In other words, seek heavenly wisdom and trample on whatever is mean. Cast aside earthly wisdom, all human recognition and self-esteem.

This is what I have told you. Buy what is cheap in place of what men find highly precious. Heavenly wisdom seems so little and so cheap that it is almost always ignored. The man who thinks highly of himself or seeks earthly praise is not wise. Many pay lip service to heavenly wisdom. Yet their actions ignore her. She is after all that pearl of great value that many do not recognise.

CHAPTER THIRTY THREE

Do Not Waver. Keep Your Mind on God

The Lord: Son, do not trust your feelings. What you feel now will easily be changed into something else. Whether you like it or not, so long as you live, you are liable to change. At one moment you are happy, at another sad. Sometimes you are at peace, other times upset. At one time you are committed, at another you are not. Now you are eager, later you are bored. At times you are heavy-hearted, then you become light hearted.

The man who is wise and well grounded in the spirit rises above these things. He pays no attention to what he feels, or from which direction the fickle wind blows. He keeps his mind on what is necessary and what helps him to reach the desired end. In this way

he can keep his mind's eye one and the same, undis-
tracted by whatever happens, directed to me.

√The clearer the mind's eye, the surer its direction
through many storms. The clarity of the mind's eye
is dimmed in many because they are too quick to turn
their attention to whatever nice thing comes their
way. Few men are found who are completely free of
the blemish of self-seeking. The Jews were the same.
They came to Martha and Mary at Bethany *not only
on account of Jesus but also to see Lazarus whom he
had raised* from the dead (Jn 12: 9). The mind's eye
must be purified. It should be sound and right. It
should be directed beyond all that comes between to
me alone.

CHAPTER THIRTY FOUR

The Lover and His Taste for God

The Servant: You are my God and my all. What more
do I want? What can I desire that is happier? How
sweet and delicious is the word to him only that loves
the Word, not the world or what is in the world! My
God and my all! He who understands needs only this
statement. The one who loves finds pleasure in its
simple repetition. When you are there, everything is
pleasant. When you are absent, everything is wearisome. You give the heart calmness, peace and festal
joy. You make us think well of everything and praise
you in everything. Without you we can find no
pleasure. Yet to be grateful and feel good we need your
grace. We need to be seasoned with the taste of your
wisdom.

Surely everything tastes right to him who tastes

you? What pleasure can he have, who does not taste you? The worldly wise lack your wisdom. They follow the tastes of the flesh. Vanity is found where the world is. Death is discovered where the flesh is. We can recognise those who are really wise. They despise worldly things and discipline the flesh. In this way they follow you. They go from vanity to truth, from the flesh to the spirit. They have a taste for God. Whatever good they find in creatures they regard as praise for the creator. The difference, the great difference between the taste of the creator and the taste of the creature is the difference between eternity and time, between the light that has no source and the light that just lights.

O eternal light, greater than all created lights! O lightning flash from above, that pierces totally my inmost heart! Purify me. Fill me with joy. Make my spirit clear and alive with your power. Make me embrace you with overwhelming joy. When shall that happy, desirable hour come when you can overwhelm me with your presence and become to me all things in all! While this gift is withheld my joy cannot be full. Alas! The old man is still alive in me. He is not fully crucified nor entirely dead. What he wants is against the spirit. He wages internal wars and prevents the reign of peace in the soul.

Yet, *you control the pride of the ocean. When its waves ride high you can calm them* (Ps 89: 10). Come to my aid. *Scatter those warmongering pagans* (Ps 68: 30). Crush them with your power. I beg you, show your greatness and the glory of your right hand. I have no other hope, no refuge, except in you, my Lord God.

CHAPTER THIRTY FIVE

Life's Ever-Present Trials

The Lord: Son, you are never safe in this life. So long
as you live, you require spiritual arms. You are among
enemies, subject to attack from left and right. If you
do not shield yourself with patience, you will soon be
wounded. Above all, keep your heart fixed on me. Be
content simply to put up with everything for my sake.
Then you will be able to stand up in the heat of the
fight. You will gain the victory of the saints. You must
be manful in your approach to everything. Be strong-
handed against everything that opposes you. To those
who prove victorious I will give manna. The lot of
the slothful will be much misery.

You may seek rest in this life. How then will you
gain rest in everlasting life? Do not expect great rest.
Expect much suffering instead. Seek true peace in
heaven, not on earth, in God alone, not in any man
nor in any other creature. The love of God should
make you put up with everything: toil and sorrow,
trials, annoyance, anxiety, restriction, weakness,
injury, detraction, criticism, humiliation, shame, correction and contempt. These are aids to virtue. They
are tests for one newly committed to Christ. They are
the things that make up the heavenly crown. I will
reward a little labour with an everlasting prize, a
shame that passes with unlimited honour.

Do you think that you can have spiritual happiness
whenever you like? My saints did not always have
this. They had many burdens, many different trials
and great discouragement. They put up with all these

things. They trusted in God more than in themselves. For they knew *that what we suffer in this life can never be compared to the glory . . . which is waiting for us* (Rom 8: 18). Do you want to have immediately what many others have barely achieved only after much tears and toil? *Put your hope in the Lord. Be strong* (Ps 27: 17). Be firm. Do not lose hope or run away. Leave your soul and body constantly open to the glory of God. The reward I pay will be very full.

CHAPTER THIRTY SIX

Men's Rash Judgement

The Lord: Son, put firm trust in the Lord. Do not fear men's judgement, so long as your own conscience shows that you are dutiful and honest. This kind of suffering is good and blessed. The truly humble person who trusts in God rather than in himself does not find such experience a hardship. Many men are great talkers. For that reason they are to be trusted less. It is not possible, however, to please everybody. The apostle Paul tried to please everyone for the glory of God. He made himself all things to all men; but it made not the slightest difference to him that any human tribunal found him worthy or not.

To the best of his ability he did what he could, simply for the edification and benefit of others. He could not avoid, however, being judged at times and even despised by others. Yet God knows everything. So Paul put everything in God's hands. Patience and humility were his defences against those lying mouths that think what is false and trivial, yet blurt out whatever they like. Now and again, however, he did reply for fear that the weak might take scandal from his silence.

What sort of man are you that you should fear mortal man? Today he is, tomorrow he is not seen. Fear God. Then you will not shudder at men's terrors. What harm can the scolding affronts of a man do to you? He does himself more harm than he does you. Whoever he is, he cannot avoid God's judgement. Keep God before your eyes and do not bicker. Whenever you seem to be beaten and blamed beyond what you have deserved, do not become upset. Do not let impatience lessen your reward. Look rather to me in heaven. I can rescue you from shame and harm. I will reward every man for whatever he does.

CHAPTER THIRTY SEVEN

Renounce Yourself and Find Freedom of Heart

The Lord: Son, leave yourself and you will come to me. Do not follow your own choice or your own self interest and you will always benefit. As soon as you give yourself to me without hesitation you will be given great grace.

The Servant: Lord, how often shall I give myself up? How can I leave myself?

The Lord: Every hour and every day, in little things and in great. There is no exception. I want to find you stripped of everything. Otherwise, how can you be mine and I yours, so long as both inwardly and outwardly you are not stripped of all self-will? The quicker you do this, the better for you. The more sincere and complete your actions are, the more pleasing you are to me and the greater will be your gain.

Some renounce themselves, yet keep back something. They do not trust God completely. At first some offer everything; but, when temptation attacks them, they go back on their offer. Such as these make very little progress in virtue. They will never achieve the real freedom of the simple heart. They will never attain the grace of pleasant intimacy with me. They must first of all renounce themselves and make me a daily offering of themselves. Without this no beneficial union exists or ever will exist.

I have told you this very often. I tell you once again. Leave yourself. Renounce yourself. You will enjoy inward peace. To possess everything you must give everything. Seek nothing. Ask no reward. To possess me you must stay with me in simple trustfulness. Your heart will be free. Darkness will not crush you. Strive for this. Pray for this. Long for this: to be stripped of all self, naked to follow the naked Jesus. Die to yourself and live eternally for me. Then day dreams, evil upsets and superfluous worries will pass away. Gone then will be excessive fear. Undisciplined love will die.

CHAPTER THIRTY EIGHT

A Good Rule of Life

The Lord: Son, you must be very careful about this. Everywhere, whatever you do, you must be inwardly free. Be self-controlled. Let everything be in your hands, not you in theirs. You must be master and controller of whatever you do. You must be a free man, not a slave. You must be a true Hebrew, heir to the lot and freedom of the sons of God. The true Hebrew stands above present things and looks to what is eternal. He has one eye on what is passing and the other on what is heavenly. He is not tempted to cling to worldly goods, but is attracted only to those things which serve him well. This is what God has ordained, what the great Craftsman has established. He has left nothing out of place in creation.

If indeed, whatever happens, you ignore outward appearances and do not examine with the eyes of the flesh whatever is seen or heard; if in any matter you go with Moses into the tabernacle and consult the Lord there, then at times you will receive the divine reply. You will be instructed concerning many things, both present and to come. Moses always went to the tabernacle to clear up his doubts and problems. When he sought relief from dangerous and wicked men, he took refuge in prayer. You too must take refuge in the cupboard of your heart. There you should ask God's aid. Josue and the sons of Israel, we read, were deceived by the Gibeonites. *They did not consult the oracle of Yahweh* (Jos 9: 14). Instead they put too much trust in sweet words. They were taken in by sham piety.

CHAPTER THIRTY NINE

Over-Eagerness

The Lord: Son, bring every problem to me. I will settle it when the time is ripe. Wait till I settle it. You will feel the benefit.

The Servant: I am quite happy to leave everything to you. I cannot really know very much. I wish I did not worry so much about things that are to come. Then I might be ready to wait on your pleasure.

The Lord: Son, a man often works hard for what he wants. When he gets it, he starts to change his mind. Desires for a particular things are seldom permanent. They move from one thing to another. It is no small matter then for a man to renounce himself even in little things.

True perfection consists in a man's denying himself. A man who has denied himself is very free and really safe. The old enemy, however, is against all good. He keeps up his temptations. Day and night he sets dangerous traps to catch the unwary in chains of deceit. *You should be awake and praying*, says the Lord, *not to be put to the test* (Mt 26: 41).

CHAPTER FORTY

Man Has No Reason to Boast

The Servant: Lord, *what is man that you should spare a thought for him, the son of man that you should care for him* (Ps 8: 4)? What has man done to earn the grace you give him? How can I complain, Lord, if you leave me? What grounds for appeal have I, if you do not do what I ask? I can with real certainty think and say: Lord, I am nothing. I can do nothing. Nothing that is entirely my own is good. I fail in every way and tend always to become nothing. Were it not for your help and the inward instruction you gave me, I would become lukewarm and cast down.

But you never change and your years are unending (Ps 102: 27). You are always good, just and holy. You do everything well, with fairness and holiness. You arrange everything wisely. As for me, I am more ready to slide back than to go forward. I never persevere in any one frame of mind. I have to go through man's seven ages. Yet things improve when you are pleased to give a helping hand. You do not need to be asked. You alone can help me and strengthen me so that I can always find more favour in your sight. (cf 1 Sam 1: 18). My heart can be turned to you alone and find rest with you.

For this reason, if I knew how to reject all human comfort, I could gain devotion and submit to that necessity which forces me to seek you. For no man will comfort me. Then I could have some reason for trusting in your grace and rejoicing in the gift of fresh comfort.

Thank you. You are the source of all that goes well for me. I am a sham and *nothing to you* (Ps 39: 5). I am weak and fickle. How can I boast or expect praise? Why should I hunger for fame? For nothing? And that indeed is most foolish. Empty honour is surely pestiferous, the most foolish thing. For it brings true honour into question and wastes the glory of heaven. A man pleased with himself displeases you. A man that gasps for praise from men is deprived of true virtue.

True honour and holy joy is to boast about you and not about self, to rejoice in your name, not in one's own strength and only for your sake to take pleasure in any created thing. May your name, not mine, be

glorified. May your work, not mine, be praised. May
your holy name be blessed. May I receive no praise
from men. You are my glory, the joy of my heart. I
glory in you and always rejoice, but *not because of
anything of my own except my weakness* (2 Cor
12: 15).

The Jews may seek the honour that one man gives
to another. I look for that which *comes from the one
God* (Jn 5: 44). All human glory, all worldly honour,
all earthly rank, compared to your everlasting glory,
is foolish and stupid. O God, my truth and my mercy!
O Blessed Trinity! To you be praise, glory, honour and
strength, world without end.

CHAPTER FORTY ONE

Despise Earthly Glory

The Lord: Son, do not sulk when you see others
honoured and promoted while you are despised and
humiliated. Turn your heart to me in heaven. Then
you will not be upset by earthly men's low opinion.

The Servant: Lord, we are blind, too ready to be
taken in by appearances. If I examine myself correctly,
I see that no creature has done me any injury that
might lead me to complain against you. Often I have
sinned very seriously against you. It is right then that
the hand of every creature should be against me.
Shame and contempt are what I really deserve. To you
be praise, honour and glory. I should be ready to be
willing to be despised, to be renounced by every
creature and to be regarded as having no worth at all.

Otherwise I cannot reach inward peace and stability. I cannot be spiritually enlightened. I cannot be fully united with you.

CHAPTER FORTY TWO

Men Do Not Bring Peace

The Lord: Son, to depend for peace on any person, either because you like him or his company, will make you unsettled and perplexed. If, however, you turn for comfort to the living everlasting truth, the death or departure of a friend will not upset you. Your love for a friend must be based on me. Whoever seems good to you and is very dear to you in this life should be loved for my sake. Without me friendship does not last and has no value. The love I do not bind together is neither real nor pure. You should, therefore, be dead to the affections of the men you have loved so that, as far as you are concerned, you can be happy to be without human companionship. A man gets nearer to God the further he moves away from all earthly comfort. The deeper he goes down into himself and the meaner he makes himself, the higher he reaches towards God.

The man who claims credit for any good in himself blocks the entrance of God's grace. The grace of the Holy Spirit always seeks out the humble heart. If you could make yourself into nothing and empty yourself of all created love, then I would have to come to you with great grace. When your attention is fixed on creatures, the attention of the Creator moves away from you. Learn total control of yourself for the sake of the creator. Then you will achieve divine knowledge. If your love and regard for even the littlest thing is undisciplined, it will hold you back from the most high and will harm you.

CHAPTER FORTY THREE

Useless Worldly Knowledge

The Lord: Son, do not be influenced by the nice subtle things men say. *The kingdom of God is not just words; it is power* (1 Cor 4: 20). Listen to my words. They put fire in the heart and light in the mind. They prompt us to repentance and bring us all sorts of comfort. Do not study even a word for the sake of appearing more learned or clever. Trying to kill your vices will do you more good than understanding many difficult problems.

Though you may have read a good deal and learned a lot, you ought nevertheless to return to the source. It is I who teach men knowledge. I give children clearer understanding than can be taught by men. When I speak to a man, he is quick to become wise. He makes good spiritual progress. Shame on those people who study the many things men find curious, but bother little about how to serve me. A time will come when Christ, the greatest master and the angels' lord, will come to test all that has been studied, that is, to examine each man's conscience. Then Jerusalem will be searched by torchlight. All that is hidden in the dark will be revealed (cf Zeph 1: 12, 1 Cor 4: 5). The tongues that argue will be still.

In a trice I lift up the humble mind to appreciate more explanations of everlasting truth than any one can have learned after ten years at the universities. I do not use words to teach. There is no welter of opinions, no bother about distinctions, no clash of disputation. I teach a man to despise what is worldly, to tire of what is passing, to seek and to taste what is lasting, to avoid honours, to put up with obstacles, to place all his trust in me, to desire nothing beyond me and to love me ardently more than anything else.

There was once a man who loved me intimately. He learned what is divine and spoke wonders. He made greater progress by leaving all than by studying niceties. To some I say ordinary things, to others special things. I show myself to some people in signs and images. To others I reveal mysteries in a flash of light. Books may say one thing; but they are not equally informative to everybody. I am the truth, the inward teacher. I examine the heart. I understand what is thought. I spur people to do things. I share out things the way I think fit.

CHAPTER FORTY FOUR

The Attraction of Outward Things

The Lord: Son, there are many things you need not know. You should think of yourself as dead to the world, as one to whom *the world is crucified* (Gal 6: 14). There are many things to which you should turn a deaf ear. You should pay more heed to those things which keep you peaceful. You are better employed to ignore what is unpleasant and leave others to think their own opinions than to become involved in argumentative rows. If you stay with God and pay attention to his judgement, you will accept defeat more easily.

The Servant: Lord, what has happened to us? We moan about temporal loss. We rush to work for small benefit. Spiritual harm is forgotten and is hardly remembered. We heed what is of little or no worth. We ignore carelessly what is most necessary. Man reaches out totally to outward things. If he does not quickly get hold of himself, he is content to stay with outward things.

CHAPTER FORTY FIVE

Credulous Careless Talk

The Servant: Lord, *help us in this hour of crisis. The help that man can give is worthless* (Ps 60: 11). How often have I found no faith where I expected it! How often have I found it where I expected it least! It is useless to trust men. The salvation of the just comes from you, O Lord. Lord, my God, may you be blessed in everything that comes to us. We are weak. We are fickle. We are quick to err and change.

Is there any man with such foresight that he guards himself in all things so that he never meets deceit or perplexity? Yet, Lord, whoever trusts in you and seeks you with a pure heart does not easily fall. Whenever he gets into trouble, no matter how entangled he may be, you are quick to rescue and console him. You never desert anyone who trusts you. It is the rare friend who stands by his friend in every difficulty. But you alone, Lord, are faithful to the end. There is none equal to you.

How wise was that holy soul who said: *My mind is fixed and grounded in Christ* (St Agatha)! If I were like that, human fear would not upset me so easily. I would not be influenced by spiky words. Who can foresee everything? Who manages to guard against those ills that are in the future? If what you expect is painful, how can the unexpected be other than really painful? Why then was I not careful? I am indeed miserable. Why was I so ready to trust others? We are men, nothing but weak men, though we may be esteemed and spoken of as angels. Whom can I trust, Lord? Whom except you? You are truth. You neither deceive nor can be deceived. Further, *no man can be relied on* (Ps 116: 11). He is weak, fickle and liable to slip, especially in words. We must not, therefore, believe immediately what seems to sound all right on the surface.

You were wise indeed to warn men against men. *A man's enemies will be those of his own household* (Mt 10: 36). We need not believe the one who said: 'Look, he is here' or: 'Look, he is there.' I have learned by my loss. I wish I might be more careful and not so foolish. Somebody said: 'Careful! Be careful. Keep to yourself what I have told you.' I keep silent and think it is a secret. Yet he cannot keep the silence he begged from me. He soon betrays both me and himself and is off. Protect me, Lord, from such stories and from careless men. I do not wish to fall into their hands and do the same things they do. Give my lips words that are reliable and true. Rid me of a slick tongue. I must avoid doing what I do not want done to me.

It is good and peaceable to be silent about others, to be slow to believe everything, not to be too ready to noise things abroad. I should reveal myself to only a few people. I should look to you always. For you look into the heart. I should not be carried away by every rumour. I should desire that whatever is inward or outward should be done in such a way as to be pleasing to your will. It is safe and preserves grace if we flee from human appearances and seek nothing which seems to be praised publicly. We should set our minds on those things which bring improvement and warmth to our life. The virtue of many has suffered because they were too well known and their virtue was too quickly praised. This frail life is a trial and a wear. What a benefit is that grace which is kept secret!

CHAPTER FORTY SIX

Trust in God When You Are Criticised

The Lord: Son, be firm. Trust in me. What are words but only words? They fly through the air. They do not harm a stone. If you are guilty, think how willing you are to make amends. If you know of no fault in you, think how willing you are to remain that way for God's sake. It is a small matter to put up with mere scolding. For you cannot bear being whipped. Surely the reason why you are so fainthearted is that you are still dependent on the flesh and pay too much attention to men. Your are afraid to be despised. You do not want your faults condemned. You want to cover up with excuses.

Have a good look at yourself. You will recognise that the world is still alive in you. You are too anxious to please men. When you take flight for fear of being humiliated and accused of your faults, this shows that you are not really humble and you are not dead to the world. *The world is not crucified* to you (Gal 6: 14). Listen to my word and you will not mind the ten thousand words men say. If even the most malicious things imaginable were said of you, what harm can they do you, provided you let it all pass over you and consider it as a speck of dust? Could any of it pull out even one of your hairs?

A man whose heart is not inward and who does not keep God before his eyes is easily worried by blame. A man who trusts in me and is not anxious to depend on his own judgement has no fear of men. I am the judge. I know every secret. I know what has happened. I know who is the offender and who is the sufferer. I have spoken. I have permitted this to happen, *so that the secret thoughts of many may be laid bare* (Lk 2: 35). I will judge the innocent and the guilty. But beforehand I will use a secret judgement to test them both.

Human witness is often mistaken. My judgement is true. It stands and will not be overturned. It is hidden for the most part. A few people are shown small parts of it. It does not err. It cannot err, no matter how incorrect it seems to the foolish. Turn to me for every judgement. Do not depend on your own opinion. The just man is not upset by whatever God causes to come to him. Even if he is accused unjustly, he does not care. He is not unduly pleased when others make excuses for him. For he realises that *it is I who search the heart and loins* (Rev 2: 23). I do not judge by face value or by human appearances. Sometimes I see as blameworthy what men judge to be worthy of praise.

The Servant: Lord God, be my strength and my guarantee. You are a just judge. You are strong and patient. You understand man's weakness and tendency to evil. My own conscience is not enough for me. You know what I do not know. I ought to have humbled myself and remained meek in the face of every rebuke. Graciously overlook the times I have not done this. Give me once more the grace of greater endurance. Your generous mercy helps me to reach forgiveness more easily than does the righteousness I imagine in myself for the defence of my hidden conscience. Even *if my conscience does not reproach me* (1 Cor 4: 4), I cannot, therefore, feel justified. For without your mercy *no one is virtuous by your standards* (Ps 143: 2).

CHAPTER FORTY SEVEN

Trial and Everlasting Life

The Lord: Son, do not let the tasks you have undertaken for me upset you. Do not let trials get you down. In all circumstances, let what I have promised strengthen and console you. I am capable of rewarding you beyond all way of measuring. Your toil here will not last long. You will not always be burdened with sorrow. Wait a while and you will see a speedy end to troubles. The time will come when toil and confusion will all cease. Whatever passes with time is but little and short.

Continue what you are doing. Work faithfully in my vineyard and I will be your wages. Write. Read. Sing. Wail. Be silent. Pray. Accept opposition with manliness. Everlasting life is worth all these battles. One day, (the Lord knows it), peace will come. Then the day and night will not be like now. That day will have light that lasts, unbounded brightness, solid peace and safe rest. Then you will not say: *Who will rescue me from this body doomed to death?* (Rom 7: 24). Nor will you cry: *Alas, too long have I lived* (Ps 120: 5). Death will be cast down. Salvation will be sure. There will be no anguish, only blessed pleasure and pleasant, well-mannered companionship.

If you had but seen the everlasting crowns of the saints in heaven! How gloriously joyful they are! In this world they were thought contemptible and not even worthy of living. You would then bow yourself to the ground. You would seek rather to be last than to come before anybody. You would not desire even life's happy days. For you would rather find pleasure in suffering for God. You would regard it as the greatest gain that men should think you worthless.

If you could but taste these things so that they could sink into your heart, you would not dare complain even once. Surely any labour can be borne for the sake of everlasting life. Is it a small matter that you might lose or gain the kingdom of God? Lift up your gaze then to heaven. Look at me and all the saints who are with me. In this world they fought a great fight. Now they rejoice. Now they are happy. Now they are safe.

Now they are at rest. Now for always they will stay with me in the kingdom of my Father.

CHAPTER FORTY EIGHT

Eternity and Our Present Trials

The Servant: O City above! O Blessed resting place! O brightest day of eternity! Night does not cloud it. The most high truth shines always in it. O day always joyful, always safe and never changing to its opposite! Would that this day had dawned and all passing things had ended. This great and splendid light has shone indeed for the saints, but pilgrims on earth see it only from afar as in a mirror.

Heaven's citizens know the joy of that day. But today is so bitter and wearisome that Eve's children groan. Earth's days are few and unhappy, full of sorrow and anguish. Man, soiled by sin, is trapped in his passions. Fearstruck, bursting with worries, his great curiosity pulls him this way and that. Uselessly entangled, bewildered by mistakes, his many labours wear him out. Temptations weigh him down. Pleasure makes him weak. Hunger torments him.

When will such evils end? When will I be free of sad bondage to vice? When, Lord, will my only thought be of you? When will I enjoy you fully? When shall I be truly free of every obstruction, without weakness of mind and body? When will peace be fixed, unruffled, safe peace that is inward and outward and secure everywhere? Good Jesus, when will I come to see you? When will I gaze on the glory of your kingdom? When will you be all in all to me? When will I be with you in that kingdom you have prepared from the beginning for those you love? I am a poor exile in enemy country, where there are daily wars and very great calamities.

Comfort my exile. Lighten my sorrow. All my desires go out to you. Everything this world offers as comfort is a burden to me. I wish to enjoy you intimately, but I cannot grasp it. I want to embrace what is heavenly, but I am weighed down with earthly worries and passions that are not yet dead in me. My mind prompts me to rise above material things, but my flesh forces me to submit. I am a luckless person. I fight with myself. I have become a burden to myself. My spirit seeks to soar, my flesh to sink.

What inward pain I suffer! While my mind is taken up with heavenly things, as I pray, a host of carnal matters rush upon me. Do not leave me, my God. *Do not repulse your servant in anger* (Ps 26: 9). Disperse these carnal things with a flash of your brightness. Shoot your arrows. Put to flight every phantasm of the enemy. Make me know you again. Make me forget what is worldly. Make me quick to reject and condemn all thoughts of sin. Help me, eternal truth, to be unmoved by foolishness. Come to me, heavenly sweetness, and let all dirtiness fly before you. Forgive me. Be merciful and kind to me. For often in my prayer I think of everything else but you. I confess that to be distracted in this way is my normal experience. Often I am not where my body stands or sits, but where I am carried in thought. Frequently my thoughts are with those things I like. What usually pleases me or normally gives me pleasure is quick to come to mind.

Therefore, O Truth, you have clearly stated: *Where*

your treasure is, there will your heart be also (Mt 6: 21). If I love heaven, I think of heavenly things. If I like the world, I rejoice in the happiness of the world and its troubles sadden me. If I love the flesh, I yearn for what is of the flesh. If I love the spirit, I am happy to think of spiritual things. Whatever then I love is what I am happy to hear and discuss. Those are the thoughts I like to take home with me. Happy that man, Lord, who for your sake takes leave of all creatures. He controls nature with firmness. His fervour of spirit helps him crucify the lusts of the flesh. He prays to you with a serene and pure conscience. He is fit to join the angel choirs. For he is free of all inward and outward concerns of this world.

CHAPTER FORTY NINE

The Reward Promised to Those Who Strive

The Lord: Son, when you realise that your desire for everlasting happiness comes from above and you want to leave the tent that is the body to be able to behold my brightness without any shadow of change, let your heart expand and accept with great longing this holy inspiration. Be totally grateful to that goodness from above, which treats you so well. It comes to you with gentleness. It rouses you to fervour. It lifts you up with strength to prevent your own weight pulling you earthwards. It is neither your own ideas nor your own efforts that give you this. It comes as a gift of grace from above because of God's regard for you. This is done so that you may make progress in virtue and in humility. Prepare yourself for greater conflicts that are to come. Seek to be united heart and mind with me. Serve me with great fervour.

Son, fires burn often; but there is no fire without smoke. Many burn with a desire for heavenly things, yet are not free of the temptation that comes from the desires of the flesh. What they do, therefore, is not simply and purely for God's honour, even though they pray to him very earnestly. Your desire is often like that. You think you are very earnest. Yet nothing is pure and perfect when it is tainted with self interest.

Do not pray for what you find pleasant and convenient. Pray rather for what I find acceptable, for what brings me glory. Right thinking should convince you that you ought to choose and follow what I want rather than what you or anybody else want. I know that you want. I have often heard you groan. You want to enjoy immediately the freedom and glory of the sons of God. The eternal dwelling and heavenly homeland fills you already with joy and pleasure. But the time has not yet come. First there must be another time, a time of war, a time of work and trial. You choose to be filled with the highest good. This cannot be reached yet. It is I. *Expect me - It is the Lord who speaks* (Zeph 3: 8) until the kingdom of God comes (cf Lk 22: 18).

You must still be tested on earth. You need much training. You will be given some comfort meantime; but complete satisfaction will be held back. *Be strong*, therefore. *Stand firm* (Deut 31: 7) as much in doing as in bearing what is against nature. You must put on the new man and be changed into another person.

Often you should do what you do not like. You should do without what you like. What pleases others brings profit. What pleases you brings little further profit. What others say shall be heard. What you say will be ignored. Others shall ask and receive. You will ask and be denied.

Men will glorify some, but will be silent about you. Others will be entrusted with this or that task. You will be regarded as good for nothing. Naturally this will upset you. You will achieve much if you bear it in silence. The servant of the Lord is normally tested in these and many similar ways to discover how much self-denial and self-effacement he can achieve. There is nothing you need to become dead to so much as seeing and suffering what is against your wishes. This is especially necessary when what you are commanded to do does not suit you and seems pointless. You are under obedience. So you dare not resist higher authority. For that reason it seems hard for you to go where another man commands and to give up your own views entirely.

Consider, however, the fruit of these labours. They do not last long, son, and their reward is great. Then you will not feel persecuted. Your patience will bring you great comfort. In return for willingly giving up a little of your wilfulness you will have what you want always in heaven. There you will find all you want, all you can ever desire. There you will find plenty of good, and no danger of losing it. There your will will be one with mine. You will desire nothing personal beyond it. There nobody will resist you or complain about you. No one will hinder or obstruct you. There all desires will be in balance. They will

satisfy your yearnings and will fulfil you completely.
There I will give glory to reward the reproach you
suffered. I will give you a cloak of praise to cover your
sorrow. I will give an everlasting kingly throne to the
one who took the last place. There the fruit of patience
shall be seen. The toil of penance shall rejoice. A
glorious crown shall reward humble submissiveness.

But now, bow under the hand of everyone. Care not
what any man said or commanded. Let this be your
greatest concern: whatever you are commanded, whatever order is given to you, whether it comes from a
superior, an inferior, or an equal, you should accept
it as totally good and try to implement it with sincerity.
One may want this, another that. One may glory in
this, another in that. Let him be praised a thousand
thousand times. For yourself, glory in neither one
thing nor the other. Be pleased that you are despised,
so long as my pleasure and honour are maintained.
You must always choose the praise of God both in life
and in death.

CHAPTER FIFTY

Submit to God in Time of Trial

PRAYER: Lord God, holy Father, may you be blessed
now and always. As you have willed it, so it has been
done. What you do is good. May your servant seek
pleasure in you, not in himself nor in any other. You
alone, Lord, are pleasure itself, my hope and my crown,
my joy and my glory. What does your servant own
that he has not received from you? He has not earned

anything. All you make and give is yours. I am wretched, *slowly dying since my youth* (Ps 88: 15). My soul is sad and near to tears, distressed at times by the passions which threaten her.

I desire the joy of peace. I beg for the peace you give your children. For you feed them in the light of your comfort. When you grant peace and pour out your joy, my soul will be filled with harmonious commitment to your praise. When, however, you leave, as you often do, she will not be able to follow your commandments. She will fall on her knees and beat her breast because things are no longer the way they were yesterday and the day before. Then your lamp shone over her head and, under the shadow of your wings, she was protected from the temptations that rushed upon her.

Just father, you are always to be praised. Your servant's hour of trial has arrived. Most lovable father, it is right that your servant suffers for your sake. Father, you are to be revered always. Now is the hour that from the beginning you have decreed would come. For a little while your servant will be outwardly oppressed; but inwardly let him live with you always. Let him be despised and humiliated for a short time. Let men see him fail. Let him be broken by suffering and weakness. In the end let him rise with you like the dawn of a new day. Let him be glorified in heaven. Holy father, this is your command. This is your will. It is done as you have commanded.

You have favoured your friend by letting him be tested here on earth and by letting him suffer for love of you. It does not matter how often and by whom you have let it be done. Nothing on earth is without purpose. You have planned and provided for everything. *It was good for me to suffer, the better to learn your statutes* (Ps 118: 71) and to cast out my heart's pride and presumption. It did me good to be covered with shame. For it made me seek solace in you rather than in men. From this I learned to fear your unchallengeable judgements. You strike the just and the wicked alike, but are still fair and reasonable.

I thank you for not sparing my ills. You have inflicted sorrow, filling me both within and without with anguish. I have no consoler under heaven except you, my Lord God. You are the heavenly doctor of souls who cures while he cuts. *You send men down to the depths of the underworld and draw them up* (Tob 13: 2). Your discipline over me and your rod shall teach me.

Look, beloved father, I am in your hands. I bend over for the rod of your correction. Beat my back and my neck. Let me bend my crookedness to your will. Make me your very humble disciple in the way that is your custom. Let me follow your every wish. I submit myself and all I have to your correction. It is better to be rebuked here than hereafter. You know every single thing. Nothing in man's conscience is hidden from you. You know what is to happen before it happens. You do not need anyone to tell you or to warn you about what is done on earth. You know what helps me to make progress. You know how much I need trial to scrub away the rust of sin. Do with me whatever your pleasure desires. Do not scorn my sinful life. There is nobody who understands it more clearly than you do.

Lord, make me know what I have to know, love

what I have to love, praise what pleases you best, value what is precious to you, condemn what your eyes abhor. Do not let me judge by outward appearances nor declare my opinion on the basis of what I hear from foolish men. Help me discern what is visible and what is spiritual. Let me always seek to know what is your will. Men are usually mistaken in their judgement. The world's lovers fail by loving only what is visible. Is a man better because men regard him more highly? When he boasts, the deceiver deceives the deceived; the empty head deceives the empty head; the blind man deceives the blind; the weak deceive the weak. And the more foolish his praise, the more he puts himself to shame. As the humble St Francis puts it: *A man is what you see he is, just that and no more.*

CHAPTER FIFTY ONE

Little Things for Big

The Lord: Son, you cannot always be keyed up with the desire for virtue. You cannot remain always on the highest rung of contemplation. Our corruptible nature makes it necessary for us to come down to earth sometimes. We must carry the weary burden of this corruptible life, whether we like it or not. While we have this mortal body we have to suffer weariness and heaviness of heart. While in the flesh we have to groan sometimes under the burdens of the flesh. For this reason we cannot cling without interruption to spiritual desires and divine contemplation.

At such times, it helps if you turn to humbler external work and refresh yourself with good deeds. Wait with trust for my coming and for my heavenly call. Be patient with your exile and mental dryness until I visit you again to free you from all your anguish. I will make you forget the toil and enjoy inward peace. I will open up to you the pleasant plains of Scripture. Then with an open heart you can begin to run the road my commandments show. You will say: *What we suffer in this life can never be compared to the glory, as yet unrevealed, which is waiting for us* (Rom 8: 18).

CHAPTER FIFTY TWO

We Do Not Deserve Comfort

The Servant: Lord, I am not fit for any comfort or for any spiritual visitation. You are fair to me when you leave me alone and helpless. Even if I shed a sea of tears, I would still be unworthy of your comfort. I deserve nothing but scourging and punishment. I have often offended you greatly. My faults are many. By strict justice, I am not worthy even of the smallest comfort. You, Lord, are kind and merciful. You do not wish your creation to perish. As a sign of the richness of your goodness and of the outpouring of your mercy, you agree to comfort your servant. This is beyond anything he deserves and beyond any human measure. Your comfort is not the same as men's empty encouragement.

What have I done, Lord, to make you give me your heavenly comfort? I do not remember having done anything good. I have always been prone to evil and slow to improve. This is true. I cannot deny it. If I were to say otherwise, you would not believe me. Nobody would back me up. What have my sins deserved except hell and eternal fire? I admit indeed that I am worthy only of scorn and of contempt. I ought not to be mentioned among your friends. Though I am sorry to hear it, I will indeed confess my sins so that I might earn more easily the opportunity to beg your mercy.

I am guilty and ashamed. What can I say? The only word my lips can utter is: I have sinned, Lord. I have sinned. Have mercy on me. Forgive me. Put up with me a little longer. Let me grieve about my sorrow before I go to the land of deep shadow that is covered with the murk of death (cf Job 10: 21). What do you demand above all from the unhappy guilty sinner? Surely that he is sorry and humble because of his faults. Humility of heart and true sorrow give birth to some hope of forgiveness. They calm the troubled conscience. They bring back the grace that was lost. They save man from the wrath that is to come. God greets the penitent soul with a holy kiss.

The humble sorrow of sinners is a suitable offering to you, Lord. It smells far sweeter to you than frankincense. It is that pleasant ointment you choose for the anointing of your feet. You never despise the heart that is humbly sorry. In it there is safety from the wrath of the enemy. There whatever was defiled and broken is cleaned and mended.

CHAPTER FIFTY THREE

Grace and Nature

The Lord: Son, my grace is precious. It does not let itself be mixed with outward things or with earthly comfort. If you wish to be filled with grace, you must reject all obstacles to grace. Seek a place that is hidden. Choose solitude. Do not ask anyone to talk to you. Pour out your devout prayers to God so that your mind may be contrite and your conscience pure. Put no value on the world. Put your concern for God before every outward concern. You cannot be involved with me and involved at the same time with pleasures that do not last. Keep your aquaintances and loved ones at a distance. Keep your mind empty of all comfort that passes. This was what the blessed apostle Peter urged us to do: to keep ourselves free as if we were visitors and pilgrims in this world (cf 1 Pet 2: 11).

If a man is not held back by love of what is in the world, how confident he will be at the time of death! The soul that is sick does not understand what it means to keep the heart detached from everything. The animal man has no appreciation of inward human freedom. Nevertheless, a man who wants to be spiritual must withdraw both from such as are far off and from such as are near to him. He must beware of no one so much as himself. If he can conquer himself, he will control other things with greater ease. Perfect victory is triumph over self. A man who controls himself so that his feelings are subject to reason and his reason obeys me in everything is a man who has conquered himself and is lord of the world.

If a man aims to reach the heights, he must be forceful at the beginning. He must place the axe firmly at the root. He must root out and destroy hidden, undisciplined self concern and all concern for private material benefit. This fault, undisciplined self love, is the hook on which hangs almost everything that has to be conquered. When this evil is conquered and controlled, great peace and lasting quiet will result. There are few, however, who strive to die to themselves or manage to reach fully beyond themselves. For this reason they remain self-involved. The spirit cannot lift them up above themselves. Whoever wishes to walk with me in freedom must deaden all his evil, undisciplined preferences. He must not cling to anything created for reasons of passion or self love.

CHAPTER FIFTY FOUR

The Movements of Grace and Nature

The Lord: Son, note carefully the movements of grace and of nature. They move subtly, but in very different ways. They are hardly ever distinguished except by a man who is spiritual and inwardly enlightened. Everybody is attracted to what is good. They strive to show some good in whatever they say or do. Many are therefore deceived by what seems to be good.

Crafty nature attracts many. She ensnares them and deceives them, always for her own ends. Grace is straightforward. She avoids all appearance of evil. She does not use deceit. Whatever she does is for God. Her purpose is to rest in God.

Nature does not want to die. She will not be held

down or conquered. She will not take second place. She is unwilling to be subject to control. Grace desires to be dead to self. She resists sensuality. She seeks to be subject and chooses to be conquered. She does not wish to use personal liberty. She desires discipline for herself and does not wish to dominate others. She longs to live, to stay and to be under God. For God's honour she is ready to give place to any human creature.

Nature works for her own benefit. She makes sure she gets any profit due to her from another. Grace is more concerned with the common good, not with what helps or benefits herself. Nature is happy to accept honourable regard. Grace faithfully gives all honour and glory to God.

Nature fears shame and contempt. Grace rejoices in *suffering humiliation for the name of Jesus* (Ac 2: 41).

Nature loves bodily rest and idleness. Grace cannot be idle. She is glad to take on work.

Nature likes to have what is curious and pretty. She hates dirty, coarse things. Grace loves what is simple and humble. She does not despise what is rough and does not mind being dressed in old rags.

Nature keeps an eye on business. She is pleased with earthly profit. She gets upset about loss and is angered by even a little affront. Grace keeps her eye on what is eternal. She does not cling to what is passing. She does not bother about losing things. Even harsh words do not make her irritable. She has laid up her treasure of joy in heaven. There nothing perishes.

Nature is greedy. She is more ready to receive than to give. She is attached to her own private property. Grace is kind and generous. She shuns private gain and is happy with little. She judges that *there is more happiness in giving than in receiving* (Ac 20: 35). Nature is fond of creatures, the body, vanity and travelling about. Grace is drawn forward to God and to virtue. She renounces creatures. She keeps herself from wandering. She is embarrassed when seen in public. Nature is glad of any outward comfort that gives pleasure to the senses. Grace seeks the comfort that only God can give. Her pleasure is in the highest good more than in any visible thing.

Anything nature does is for her own gain and benefit. She can do nothing for nothing. She hopes to get in return for her good deed either the same or better, either praise or a favour. She is eager that her deeds and her gifts should be well appreciated. Grace expects no temporal reward and asks for no payment other than God alone. Furthermore, she looks for life's necessities only in so far as they help her reach what is eternal.

Nature loves to have many friends and neighbours. She boasts of her high rank and noble birth. She is obsequious with the powerful. She flatters the rich. She praises herself and anybody like her. Grace loves her enemies and takes no pride in her crowds of friends. She bothers neither about rank nor about birth, except when they have greater virtue. She prefers the poor to the rich. She has more pity for the innocent than for the powerful. She shares her joy more with the true than with the false. She encourages the good to go after more of God's gifts and to imitate the virtues of the Son of God.

Nature is quick to complain about want and hardship. Grace bears want with patience.

For nature, everything revolves round herself. She fights for her own and pleads in her own favour. Grace returns everything to God from whom it all came. She credits herself with nothing. She is not arrogant in what she expects. She does not argue. She does not prefer her own opinion to that of others. She makes her opinion and understanding take second place to God's wisdom and judgement.

Nature likes to hear news and know things that are secret. She likes to go out and gain first hand experience of many things. She likes to be acclaimed. She does those things which gain her praise and admiration. Grace is not concerned with knowing the curious and the novel. All such things arise out of the old corruption. After all, there is nothing new or lasting on earth. She shows men how to curb the senses, how to avoid foolish self-satisfaction and swank. She teaches men to cover up those things that earn praise and admiration. She teaches men to use everything and all knowledge in the search for the fruit that is profitable, the praise and honour of God. She does not wish that she herself or what she owns be praised. She chooses to bless God for all the gifts he has given us in simple charity.

Grace is a supernatural light, a special gift of God. She is the special sign of those who are chosen and the pledge of eternal salvation. She lifts a man up from earthly things so that he loves what is heavenly. She makes the carnal man spiritual. The more a man controls and overcomes nature, the greater the grace that flows into him. By fresh daily contact with God the inward man is remade in God's image.

152

The Power of Grace

The Servant: My Lord God, you have made me an image and likeness of yourself. Grant me the grace which you have shown to be necessary for salvation. I wish to conquer what is worst in my nature. For it attracts me to sin and to perdition. In my body I feel the law of sin contradicting the law of my mind. It enslaves me and makes me sensual in many ways. Without the help of your grace, flowing hot in my heart, I cannot resist lust.

I need your grace, great grace indeed. From my youth I have been ready to do evil. By the fall of Adam, the first man, nature has been tainted. The punishment of that stain has come upon all men. Although the nature you created was good and proper, this nature has become a sign of sin and of the corruption of nature itself. The result is that, left to itself, nature is attracted to what is mean and wicked. The little strength that remains is like a spark hidden among ashes. Now, natural reason, clouded with darkness, is still able to recognise good and evil, the gap between truth and falsehood. Unable to do all that it would like to do, it enjoys no longer the full light of truth or healthy affections.

For this reason, my God, *in my inmost self I dearly love (your) law* (Rom 7: 22). I know that your command is good, just and holy. I know that evil is to be condemned and sin is to be avoided, *I who serve in my unspiritual self the law of sin* (Rom 7: 25). I obey sensuality instead of reason. *Though the will to do*

good is in me, the performance is not (Rom 7: 18).
Often I start to do good things. Yet, because I lack your
grace, when I meet a little opposition, I shrink back
and give up. I know the way to perfection. I see clearly
what has to be done. What actually happens is this.
I am pressed down by the weight of my corruption
and do not achieve perfection.

Lord, I have the greatest need of your grace. I need
it to begin anything good, to continue it and to finish
it. Without your grace I can do nothing. With the
help of your grace I can do anything. O Grace that
really comes from heaven, without you I can have no
personal merit. Without you my natural gifts are
valueless. Without grace no skills, no riches, no beauty,
no strength, no cleverness, no eloquence have any
value before God. The gifts of nature are the common
possession of both the good and the bad. The gift
which is proper to those who are chosen is grace or
love. It is their hallmark and is the reason why they
are judged worthy of eternal life. This gift of grace is
so excellent that the gift of prophecy, the working of
miracles and outstanding discernment are of no value
without it. Faith, hope and any other virtue are unac-
ceptable to you if they lack charity and grace.

O very blessed grace! You make the poor in spirit
rich in virtues. You give deep humility to whoever is
rich in virtues. Come. Come down to me. In the
morning, fill me with comfort so that my soul does
not falter through weariness and spiritual dryness.
Lord, I beg you to see fit to let me have grace. For *my
grace is enough for you* (2 Cor. 12: 9), even if I do not
get what nature desires. When I have your grace, I
fear no evil, even though I might be tempted and

harried by many trials. Your grace is my strength. She gives me advice and help. She is more powerful than any man and wiser than any sage.

She is the mistress of truth, the teacher of discipline, light to the heart, relief from what presses us down, the banisher of sadness, the remover of fear, the nurse of commitment, the drawer of tears. What am I without her? I am but a dry stick, a useless stump, fit to be thrown away. *Lord God, open our hearts to your grace. Let it go before us and be with us so that we may always be intent on doing your will* (Collect of the 28th Week in Ordinary Time).

CHAPTER FIFTY SIX

Self-Denial and the Cross

The Lord: Son, the further you can get away from yourself, the nearer you can get to me. Just as you achieve inward peace when you desire nothing that is outward, so the more inwardly you are cut off from yourself the closer is your union with God. I want you to learn to surrender yourself entirely to my will without objection or complaint. Follow me. *I am the Way, the Truth and the Life* (Jn 14: 6). Without the Way there is no journey. Without the Truth there is no knowledge. Without Life there is no living. I am the way you should follow. I am the truth you should believe. I am the life you should trust. I am the unbreakable way, the infallible truth, the unending life. I am the straightest way, the highest truth, the real way, the blessed uncreated way. If you keep my way you will know the truth. The truth will free you so that you can grasp eternal life.

If you wish to enter into life, keep the commandments (Mt 19: 17). If you wish to know the truth, trust me. *If you wish to be perfect, go and sell what you own* (Mt 19: 21). *If anyone wants to be a follower of mine, let him renounce himself* (Mt 16: 24). If you wish to possess the life that is blessed, despise the life that is present. If you wish to be lifted up to heaven, humble yourself on earth. If you wish to reign with me, carry your cross. Only the servants of the cross will find the way to happiness and real light.

The Servant: Lord Jesus, your life was difficult. You were despised in the world. Let me follow you by being despised in the world. *The disciple is not superior to his teacher nor the slave to his master* (Mt 10: 24). Train your servant in your life. For my salvation and real holiness are there. Whatever I study or hear beyond this brings me neither refreshment nor delight.

The Lord: You know and have studied all this. You will be blessed if you do it. *Anybody who receives my commandments and keeps them will be the one who loves me . . . and I shall love him and show myself to him* (Jn 14: 21). I shall let him sit with me in the kingdom of my Father.

The Servant: Lord Jesus, this is what you have said and promised. So let it be done. But let me earn it. I have accepted it. I have indeed accepted the cross from your hand. I will carry it. I will carry it until death, just as you put it on me. The life of a good monk is indeed a cross, but it leads to heaven. Now that I have started, I may not go back and I should not give up. Come, brothers, let us go together with Jesus as our companion. We accept this cross because of Jesus. We will persevere with the cross because of Jesus. He will be our helper. He has led the way ahead of us. Look, our king goes before us. He has fought for us. Let us follow with courage. Let no one fear what is terrible. Let us be ready to battle courageously and to die, *and leave nothing to tarnish our reputation* (1 Mac 9: 10). Let us not flee from the cross.

CHAPTER FIFTY SEVEN

Patience with our Lapses

The Lord: Son, when times are hard, patience and humility please me more than great consolation and devotion when times are easy. Why do you become upset by the least thing said against you? If even greater things had been said against you, you ought not to have been upset. Let it pass for the present. It is not the first time. It is nothing new. It will not be the last time if you live much longer. As long as there is no opposition you are courageous enough. At such times, you are a good counsellor. You know how to persuade others to be strong. Yet, when sudden trial comes to your own door, you lose your own counsel and strength. Take note of your great weakness. You experience it often in small matters. It is for the sake of your salvation that these and similar things come to you.

Put it out of mind as best you know how. Yet, if the problem touches you very closely, do not be upset or perplexed. Suffer it at least with patience if you cannot accept it with joy. If you hear what you do not like and feel indignant about it, control yourself. Do not let an ill-considered word pass your lips. Such things are a scandal to children. Your indignation will soon calm down. Grace will come back and sweeten the sorrow that was bottled up inside you. I am still alive, says the Lord. I am ready to support you and comfort you more than before. But you must trust me and call on me with devotion.

Take courage and get ready to endure more. Everything is not lost because you are upset and have strong temptations. You are a man, not God. You are a body, not an angel. How can you expect always to stay virtuous? Not even the angels in heaven or the first man in paradise managed that. It is I who comfort those who mourn. I bring those who know their weakness into the protection of my godhead.

The Servant: Lord, may your word be blessed. It is sweeter to me than honey or the honeycomb. I am greatly tried. I am full of anxiety. How could I manage without the comfort of your holy instruction? As long as I reach the gate of salvation, why should I worry about the sufferings I have to undergo? Grant me a happy end. Grant me a happy passage out of this world. Remember me, Lord. Show me the right way to your kingdom. Amen.

CHAPTER FIFTY EIGHT

The Secret of God's Judgements

The Lord: Son, be careful not to argue about things beyond your ken, particularly the hidden judgements of God, such as: why one man is left alone and another receives much grace; why one man has so much sorrow and another such excessive pleasure. Such matters are beyond human grasp. Neither reason nor argument have any place in the investigation of God's judgement. Whenever the enemy suggests this or curious men inquire about it, give them the prophet's reply: *Righteous indeed, Yahweh! and all your rulings correct!* (Ps 119: 137). Further: *The judgements of Yahweh are true, righteous every one* (Ps 19: 9). My judgements are to be feared, not discussed. They are beyond the understanding of men.

Do not argue and dispute about the merits of the saints. Was this one more holy or that one greater in the kingdom of heaven? Such talk breeds strife and useless argument. It also nurtures pride and conceit. When one man strives to promote one saint and another to honour another saint, this can be a source of bickering and rows. Wishing to know and study such matters is quite a fruitless occupation. Moreover, it is displeasing to the saints. I am, after all, not the God of rows, but the God of peace. This peace is found in real humility, not in getting one over your neighbour.

Devotion prompts some to love one saint more than another. Such devotion is more human than divine. It was I who made the saints. I provided the grace. I granted the glory. I know the merits of each, I supported them with sweet blessings. Before the world began I knew those I have loved. I chose them on earth. They did not choose me first. My grace called them. My mercy attracted them. I was their leader when temptation came. I gave them excellent comfort. I granted them perseverance and I rewarded their patience.

I know them thoroughly. I embrace them with immeasurable love. I am to be praised in all my saints. I am to be blessed above all and honoured in every one of these whom, though they had done nothing beforehand that might merit it, I have glorified and chosen. The man who makes little of the least of my saints does no honour to the greatest. For I made both the little and the great. Whoever belittles any saint belittles me and all others in the kingdom of heaven. They are all together bound in one chain of charity. They are one in thought. They are one in will and one in their hope for one another.

What is more important, they love me more than themselves, more than all their merits. They are lifted out of themselves, pulled beyond self-love. So they all surge towards love of me in whom they find joyful peace. Nothing can hold them back or turn them aside from this. Filled with eternal truth, they burn with the fire of unquenchable charity. Let carnal, animal men stop discussing the rank of the saints. Their only skill is to know their own private pleasure. They add or subtract what they like, not what the eternal truth likes.

Many of them are ignorant, especially those who have little enlightenment and have never experienced any perfect spiritual love. Many more are attracted by natural affection and human friendship towards men of some sort or another. They fancy that they can behave in heaven in much the same way as they behave on earth. But there is a huge difference between what imperfect people think and what is contemplated by those who have been enlightened by heavenly revelation.

Beware then, Son; do not be curious and discuss what is beyond your understanding. Make it your business and concern to be even the least in the kingdom of God. Let us suppose someone knew who was holier and greater in the kingdom of God. How could that knowledge help him? The only help would be to make him more humble in my presence and to make him praise my name. God thinks most highly of the man who reflects on his great sins, his small virtue and the distance that separates him from the perfection of the saints. Such a man is more acceptable to God than the one who argues whether one saint is greater or smaller than another. It is better to pray to the saints with devout tears and beg their prayers with humble mind than to inquire with fruitless curiosity into their secrets.

The saints are perfectly happy. Would that men knew how to be happy and stop chattering. The saints do not boast about what they deserve. They claim no credit for their goodness. Instead they give me the credit. In my unmeasurable love, I have given them everything. They are so full of pleasure in the godhead that they themselves are short of neither glory nor happiness. The higher the glory of the saints, the humbler they are in themselves, the nearer they are to me and the better I love them. Therefore it is written: They cast down their crowns before God, they fell face down before the Lamb and they adored the one who lives forever (cf Rev 5).

Many ask who is greater in the kingdom of God. They do not know whether they themselves can be counted among the least. It is a great thing to be least in heaven. For all are great in heaven. They are all called the children of God. They are indeed. *The least among you will become a clan* (Is 60: 62). *To live to be a hundred will be a sign of a curse* (Is 65: 20). When the disciples asked who would be greater in the kingdom of heaven, this was the reply they got: *Unless you change and become like little children you will never enter the kingdom of heaven. And so the one who makes himself as little as this little child is the greatest in the kingdom of heaven* (Mt 18: 3-4).

Shame on those who are unwilling to be as humble as little children. The humble gate of the kingdom of heaven will not grant them entry. Shame on the rich. They have their comfort here. When the poor enter the kingdom of God the rich shall weep outside. Rejoice, you who are humble. Be happy, you who are poor. If you do what is right, you will own the kingdom of God.

CHAPTER FIFTY NINE

Hope and Trust in God

The Servant: Lord, what kind of trust can I have in this life? Of all that is under heaven, what gives me

the greatest comfort? Surely only you, Lord God? Your
mercy is given totally, not shared. Where would I be
without you? If you are there, how can I be harmed?
I prefer poverty for you than riches without you. I
would rather be with you as an exile on earth than
own heaven without you. Where you are is heaven.
Where you are not is hell and death. You are what I
desire. I have to sigh for you, cry for you and pray to
you. I can rely on nobody except only you, my God.
You are ready to help me when I need help. You are
my hope, my trust, my consoler. I can depend on you
for everything.

All the rest seem more interested in themselves (Phil
2: 21). You are my salvation. You alone make progress
possible for me. You make everything good for me.
You expose me to many temptations and some opposition. Yet you control everything for my benefit. For
it is your custom to use a thousand means of testing
those you love. You are to be loved and praised when
you send me trials as well as when you fill me with
heavenly comfort.

I take refuge in you, Lord. I place all my trust in
you. I leave my trial and anguish in your care. I find
that whatever I see outside of you is weak and fickle.
Crowds of friends are useless. Hosts of helpers cannot
aid me. Wise counsellors cannot answer for me. The
books of the learned give me no comfort. No wealth
can free me. No secret place of beauty can keep me
safe. None of these are of any use unless you are
present to assist, to support, to instruct and to guard
me. All that seems to bring peace or happiness is
nothing without you. When you are absent, they
bring no real happiness. You are the perfection of all

that is good, the highest thing in life, the deepest thing that can be said. Hoping in you is the greatest comfort your servants can have.

My eyes are turned to you, Lord God. My trust is in you, father of mercy. Bless my soul and make it holy with your heavenly blessing. Let it be a holy dwelling and an everlasting seat for your glory. May you find nothing offensive to your majestic eyes in this temple of your dignity. May your regard for me be as great as your goodness, as frequent as your mercy. I, your servant, am under the shadow of death. Listen to my prayer. I, your little servant, am caught in the dangers of this corruptible life. Protect me and keep me strong. Let your grace be my companion and guide me along the way of peace to the homeland of life that is everlasting.

164

BOOK FOUR

THE SACRAMENT OF THE ALTAR

(A Devout Exhortation concerning Holy Communion)

Christ says: *Come to me all you that labour and are overburdened, and I will give you rest* (Mt 11: 28), says the Lord.

The bread that I will give is my flesh for the life of the world (Jn 6: 51).

Take it and eat, this is my body (Mt 26: 26) *which is for you; do this as a memorial of me* (1 Cor 11: 24).

He who eats my flesh and drinks my blood lives in me and I live in him (Jn 6: 56).

The words I have spoken to you are spirit and life (Jn 6: 63).

CHAPTER ONE

Reverence and Communion

The Disciple Says: Christ, these are your words. You did not say them all at the one time. They are not written in the one place. Yet they are eternally true. I must accept them with faithful thanks because they are really yours. You said these words. So they are yours. You said them for my benefit. So they are also mine. I accept them gladly from your lips. May they sink deep into my heart. Such words of sweet and loving piety fill me with excitement. Yet my own sins terrify me. My own impure conscience pushes me back from accepting these great mysteries. The sweetness of your words attracts me. My many vices weigh me down.

You bind me in faith to approach you whenever I wish to be with you to share the food of immortality and to reach the glory of everlasting life. *Come to me all you that labour and are overburdened, and I will give you rest* (Mt 11: 28). Your word is sweet in the ear of the sinner. Lord, my God, you have invited the poor and the needy to the communion of your most holy body. Lord, how can I dare come to you? Yet you say: *Come to me all you* ... (Mt 11: 28).

What is the meaning of this loving consideration and friendly invitation? How can I dare approach you? I am unaware of any good in me, which could give me reason to do so. How can I bring you into my house? I have so often been an offense in your gracious sight. Angels and archangels revere you. Saints and holy men fear you. Yet you say: *Come to me all you* ... (Mt 11: 28). If you yourself, Lord, had not said it, nobody would have believed it. If you had not commanded it, nobody would dare come to you.

Noah was a good man. He worked a hundred years to make the ark to save himself and just a few. How can I get ready in one hour to receive with reverence the maker of the world?

Your great servant, Moses, was your special friend. He made an ark of incorruptible wood and covered it with purest gold so that he could place in it the tables of the law. I am a corrupt creature. How can I dare to receive with carelessness the maker of the law and the giver of life?

Solomon was the wisest king of Israel. He spent seven years building a magnificent temple in your honour. He celebrated its dedication for eight days. He made a thousand peace offerings. He brought the ark of the covenant with joyful trumpet blast to the place he had prepared.

How can I, unhappy me, the poorest of men, how can I dare bring you into my house? I can hardly spend a half an hour in prayer. Would that even once I could spend a half an hour worthily!

Solomon, Moses and Noah tried to do so much to please you, my God. Alas! How little do I do! I spend such a short time preparing for communion. Yet these holy patriarchs and prophets, kings and princes showed so much love for the worship of God.

King David, the most devout king, danced with all his might before the ark of God to commemorate the blessings given to his ancestors. He fashioned different types of instruments. He composed psalms. He sang them joyfully, often to the accompaniment of the harp. He taught the people of Israel to praise God with all their hearts, to join their voices daily in the praise and blessing of God. If, in those days, such devoted effort was made to recite the praise of God in the presence of the ark of the covenant, how much more reverent devotion should I and all christian people have in the presence of the sacrament in which we receive the most excellent body of Christ?

Many rush to different places to visit the relics of the saints. They are astounded by the stories of what the saints did. They gape at their great churches. They kiss their holy bones wrapped in gold and silk. Yet there you are in front of me on the altar, my God, the most holy, man's creator and the angels' lord. The men who gaze on the relics of the saints are drawn there often by curiosity and the novelty of seeing what they never saw before. If they run from place to place, but have no real sorrow for their sins, they can claim little benefit or improvement at their return home. Here in the sacrament of the altar, my Lord God and Man Jesus Christ, you are wholly present. As often as you are received with worthy devotion, you bring us plenty of benefit and improvement. What draws us to the altar is not levity or curiosity or feeling. It is strong faith, firm hope and true charity.

O God, unseen maker of the world, you do wonderful things for us. You are kind and gracious to those you love. For you offer them yourself in the sacrament. This is beyond understanding. It attracts those who are especially devout. It lights the fire of love in them. Those who seek perfection in their whole lives are your true friends. This most wonderful sacrament brings them the grace of great devotion and a great love of virtue.

The grace of this sacrament is so wonderfully hidden that only Christ's faithful know it. Those who are faithless slaves to sin cannot experience it. This sacrament gives spiritual grace. It restores the virtue that the soul has lost. It renders beautiful what has been marred by sin. Its grace is sometimes so great that the perfection of devotion flows beyond the spirit, and even the body feels it has been given an increase in strength.

It is regrettable and a pity that we are so lukewarm and so careless. We should be persuaded to receive Christ with greater affection. He is our only hope of salvation and merit. He makes us holy and redeems us. He grants comfort on earth to us and everlasting benefit to the saints. It is even more regrettable that so many have so little understanding of this saving mystery. For it gives such joy in heaven and such support throughout the world. How blind and hard hearted men are! They care so little for this indescribable gift. They are so used to it that they ignore it.

If this holy sacrament was celebrated in only one place and consecrated by only one priest in the world, can you imagine how anxiously men would gather in that one place round that one priest to see the holy mysteries celebrated? Now there are many priests. Christ is offered in many places to show the grace more clearly, to demonstrate God's love for men, the more widely holy communion is distributed throughout the world.

Thank you, Jesus, my God, eternal shepherd. You have consented to refresh poor exiled men with your precious body and blood. You have invited us to receive these mysteries with your very own words: *Come to me all you that labour and are overburdened, and I will give you rest* (Mt 11: 28).

CHAPTER TWO

Communion: The Sign of God's Love

The Disciple Says: Lord, I rely on your goodness and

mercy. Weak, I come to my saviour. Hungry and thirsty, I approach the spring of life. Needy, I come to the king of heaven, a slave to my Lord, a creature to my creator, comfortless to my kind comforter. Why should you come to me? Who am I to deserve the gift of you? How can a sinner dare to appear before you? You know your servant. You know he owns nothing that is good or might make you give him anything. I confess my meanness. I recognise your goodness. I praise your kindness. I thank you for your great love. It is you who make me do this, not my own merits. You do this to show more clearly your goodness to me, to make me share charity more deeply, to make me admire humility more perfectly. This is your pleasure. This is what you have commanded. I too am pleased that you show such consideration. Would that my sinfulness did not stand in the way.

O sweet and loving Jesus, we have received your sacred body. What reverent thanks and endless praise are your due! No man yet has been able to express its value. What then can I think of this communion in which my Lord comes to me? I cannot reverence him as I should. Yet I have great desire to receive him. What better and more wholesome thing can I imagine except to humble myself totally before you and praise your boundless goodness to me.

I praise you, Lord God. I glorify you for ever. I despise myself. I place myself at your feet, deeply aware of my meanness. You are the most holy. I am the worst of sinners. You turn to me. I am not fit to look at you. You come to me. You want to be with me. You invite me to your banquet. You want to feed me with heavenly food, the bread of angels, nothing else but yourself, the living bread *which comes down from heaven and gives life to the world* (Jn 6: 33).

You are the spring of love. Your consideration shines out. Your loving consideration ought to earn you thanks and praise. How good, how profitable was the wisdom that made you institute this sacrament! What a sweet and pleasant banquet! You are the food it provides. What a wonderful thing you have done! What strength is in your power! How indescribable your truth! You spoke, and everything was done. It was done just as you commanded.

It is wonderful, beyond human understanding, yet worthy of belief, that you, my Lord God, are contained completely in the slight appearances of bread and wine. You are not destroyed when you are eaten by those who receive you. You are the Lord of all. You lack nothing. Yet it is your will to stay with us through your sacrament. Keep my heart and body pure so that I can often celebrate your mysteries with clear and happy conscience. Let me reach everlasting salvation through these mysteries. You have instituted them as a sacred everlasting memorial of your glory.

Be glad, my soul. Give thanks to God for this glorious gift, the wonderful comfort he has left us in this valley of tears. Whenever you think about this mystery and receive the body of Christ, you share in the merits of Christ. For you take part in the work of your own redemption. Christ's charity is never diminished. There can be no limit to the greatness of his sacrifice. You should, therefore, approach this mystery of salvation with freshness of mind and with constant attention. When you celebrate or hear Mass, it should seem as great, fresh and pleasant to you as if it were the very day when Christ first entered the Virgin's womb and was made flesh, or when Christ suffered and died for men, hanging on the cross.

CHAPTER THREE

Frequent Communion

The Disciple Says: Look, Lord, I am coming to you. I wish your gift to make me good. I wish to be gladdened by the banquet which *you in your goodness, God, provided for the needy* (Ps 68: 10). All I can or should wish is in you. You are my salvation and redemption, my hope and my strength, my good name and my honour. Today, therefore, *give your servant reason to rejoice, for to you, Lord Jesus, I lift my soul* (Ps 86: 4). I wish to receive you with reverent devotion. I wish to bring you into my house. I want, like Zacchaeus, to be blessed by you. I want to be remembered among the children of Abraham. My soul desires your body. My heart wants to be one with you.

Give yourself to me and I will be satisfied. Besides you there is no comfort. I cannot be without you. If you do not come to me, I cannot live. I should, therefore, come to you often. I should use you as a medicine for my salvation. Do not let me fall by the wayside. Do not let me be deprived of this heavenly nourishment. Most merciful Jesus, when you preached to the people and cured many, you once said: *I do not want to send them off hungry, they might collapse on the way* (Mt 15: 32). Treat me in the same way, you who have left yourself in your sacrament for the comfort of those who believe in you. You are the sweet refreshment of the soul. Whoever receives you worthily shares the inheritance of eternal glory. I am a toiling sinner, quick to fall and grow lukewarm. I need then to renew myself by frequent prayer, confession and the communion of your sacred body. For, if I omit these too much, I might fail in my holy resolution.

A man's heart contrives evil from his youth (cf Gen 8: 21). Without the help of the divine medicine he is liable quickly to choose what is worse. Holy communion pulls him back from evil and gives him the strength to do good. Too often I am careless and lukewarm when I receive communion or celebrate Mass. What will become of me if I do not take this medicine and do not seek to benefit from the great help it gives? Even if I am not fit and prepared to celebrate Mass daily, I should make an effort to receive the divine mysteries at suitable times. I should present myself for a share in this great grace. This is the main comfort provided for the faithful soul that journeys in this mortal body. To keep God before his mind, he should often receive his beloved with devotion.

What wonderfully loving consideration you show us! You, Lord God, the creator who gives life to every spirit, consent to come to the poor little soul. You fill her hunger with your whole godhead and humanity. O lucky heart and blessed soul, made worthy to receive devoutly her Lord God and to be filled with gladness of spirit! What a great Lord she receives! What a delightful guest is her visitor! What a pleasant companion she welcomes! What a faithful friend she receives! What a beautiful noble spouse she embraces!

He must be loved above all who are loved and above all that is desired. My most delightful friend, let heaven and earth and all their glory be silent before you. Whatever reasons they have for praise and honour are your gracious gifts. They will not equal, however, the glory of your name. For your understanding is infinite (cf Ps 147: 5).

CHAPTER FOUR

The Benefits of Communion

The Disciple Says: Lord, my God, help your servant *with your choicest blessings* (Ps 21: 2). Then I might be fit to come to your magnificent sacrament with proper devotion. Rouse my heart. Banish my weary torpor. *Come to me as a saviour* (Ps 106: 4). Let me taste your sweetness of spirit, hidden in this sacrament like a spring that is full. Give my eyes the power to look on this great mystery. Strengthen my faith to believe it. What you have done is something beyond human power. You did it. It was not thought up by man. By his own efforts man cannot grasp or understand these things that reach beyond the understanding of the angels. How, therefore, can an unworthy sinner, dust and muck that he is, grasp and study such a sacred secret?

Lord, I come to you in reverent hope. My heart is simple. My faith is good and strong. I follow your command. I believe that you are really here in this sacrament both as God and as man. I wish to receive you and to join myself to you in charity. I ask, therefore, for your clemency and beg you to give me the special grace that brings this about. I want to melt completely in the flood of love. Do not let me ever again be filled with any other comfort. This most high and worthy sacrament is the salvation of both soul and body. It is the medicine for every spiritual ailment. It cures my vices. It curbs my appetites. It conquers or weakens temptations. It fills us up with greater grace. By it virtue that is once begun is increased; faith is made firm; hope is made strong; charity is set alight and made expand.

In this sacrament, you have given and continue to give many good things to those you love when they receive communion with devotion. You are my God, my soul's guardian. You support man in his weakness. You are the giver of every inward comfort. You give men great comfort as an antidote to different troubles. You lift them out of their depression so that they trust in your protection. You give them inward light and refreshment by a new grace so that, though before communion they felt worried and without feeling, afterwards, refreshed with heavenly food and drink, they find themselves changed for the better. You do this to those you love so that they can really recognise and experience clearly the extent of their own weakness, the amount of grace and goodness you give them. In themselves they are cold and hard. They lack devotion. Through you they manage to become fervent, eager and devout. If a man comes humbly to the well of sweetness, how can he not carry away at least a little sweetness? If a man stands close to a great fire, will he not gain at least a little warmth from it? You are the source that is full and overflowing. You are the fire that burns and never goes out.

If I may not draw from the source of the well and drink my fill, I will at least put my lips to its trickle. There I will quench my thirst with a few drops and I will not be entirely dried out. I may not be able to be wholly heavenly and on fire like the cherubim and seraphim. All the same I will seek with earnest devotion to make my heart ready by humbly receiving this life giving sacrament. Then I may burn with at least a little of the divine flame. Good Jesus, most holy saviour, you consent to invite everyone to you. With gracious kindness supply what I lack. *Come to me all you that labour and are overburdened, and I will give you rest* (Mt 11: 28).

I toil with sweating brow. I am tormented with grief. I am weighed down with sin. Temptations upset me. Evil desires confuse and oppress me. *I have no one to help me* (Ps 22: 11), no one to release me and make me safe except you, Lord God, my saviour. I give you me and all I have. Guard me, and guide me to everlasting life.

You have given me your body and blood for food and drink. Accept me for the sake of your praise and glory. Grant, Lord God, my saviour, that I may often receive your mystery and grow in devotion and love.

CHAPTER FIVE

The Dignity of the Priest

The Disciple Says: If you were pure as an angel and

holy as St John the Baptist, you would still be unfit to receive or handle this sacrament. Man has not earned any right to hold and consecrate the sacrament of Christ or to take as food the bread of angels. How great the ministry and dignity of the priest! He is appointed to do what angels may not do. Only priests properly ordained by the Church have the power to celebrate and consecrate the body of Christ. The priest is the minister. He uses God's words. He follows God's command and institution. It is God, however, who is the principal author, the unseen doer. Everything he wants is subject to him. He brings about all that he has commanded.

Concerning this most excellent sacrament you should trust in God more than in any outward sign or any understanding of our own. We must approach it, therefore, with fearful reverence. Take care for yourself. Be aware whose ministry has been given to you by the laying on of the bishop's hand. You have become a priest. You are consecrated to celebrate Mass. Be aware that you are to offer sacrifice to God at the proper time and with devoted faithfulness. You are to show yourself blameless. You have not lightened your burden. You are now bound by a tighter chain of discipline. You are committed to reach for a greater perfection of holiness. A priest should be endowed with every virtue. He should be an example of good life to others. He should not concern himself with the ordinary common things of men. His concern should be with heaven's angels and those who are perfect on earth.

The priest in sacred vestments takes the place of Christ. He should pray to God with humble constancy for himself and for all men. He carries the sign of the Lord's cross before and behind himself, a constant reminder of Christ's sufferings. He wears the cross in front of the chasuble to keep constantly before his eyes the footsteps of Christ, in which he desires fervently to walk. He is signed with the cross on his back so that he may carry cheerfully in God's name whatever others impose on him. He keeps the cross in front of him to remind him of his own sins. He carries the cross on his back to realise that he must weep with sympathy for the sins of others. For he is appointed to stand between the sinner and God. His desire to become fit to win God's grace and mercy should be such that he is not slow to pray or offer the holy sacrifice. When the priest celebrates Mass, he honours God, he gives joy to the angels, he builds up the Church, he gives aid to the living and he brings rest to the dead. He gives himself a share in all that is good.

CHAPTER SIX

Preparation for Communion

The Disciple Says: When I balance my own meanness against your dignity, Lord, I really shudder. I am filled with confusion. Not to come to you is to fly from life. To come to you unworthily is to cause offense. What am I to do, my God, my helper and my adviser in times of difficulty?

Show me the right way. Give me a short exercise suitable for holy communion. It is useful to know how I must prepare my heart with devoted reverence to receive your sacrament properly, to celebrate your great divine sacrifice.

CHAPTER SEVEN

Examination of Conscience

The Beloved Says: First and foremost, God's priests should approach the celebration, handling and receiving of communion with deep humility, prayerful reverence, strong faith and a holy mind fixed on the glory of God. Examine your conscience carefully. As far as you can, make it sparklingly clean by confessing your sins with really humble sorrow. Nothing should weigh on your conscience. Nothing you know should give you remorse or stop you coming freely. Be sorry for all your sins, but grieve and groan particularly for your daily faults. When you have the opportunity, confess to God in the quiet of your heart every miserable thing that lust promotes in you.

Lament with sorrow that you are still carnal, worldly, not dead to lust, but full of the desires of the body. Your outward feelings are so unguarded. Your mind is so often confused by empty daydreams. You are so concerned with what is outward and so careless of what is inward. You are so ready to laugh and be frivolous, yet so slow to tears and sorrow. You are so anxious for bodily ease and convenience, so uninterested in strictness and fervour. You are so curious to hear what is new and see what is nice, but unwilling to embrace what is lowly and mean. You are so greedy

for getting, so sparing in giving, so tenacious in keep-
ing. You are so careless in speech, so unready for
silence. You are so ill mannered, aggressive, greedy for
food, deaf to God's word. You are so ready to rest, so
slow to work. You listen avidly to stories, but sleep
through holy vigils. You are so quick to get things
over, so wandering in attention, so careless in reciting
the office, so lukewarm in celebrating Mass, so
unmoved by communion. You are quickly distracted,
seldom fully recollected. Your anger is sudden, your
displeasure easily incurred. You are so quick to judge,
so severe in your condemnation. You are so glad to be
prosperous, so weak when you are in difficulties. You
are so full of good ideas, yet so empty of any real
action.

When you have confessed with sorrow these and
your other faults, when you have deplored with great
disgust your own weakness, make a firm resolution to
better your life and seek improvement. Be resigned
and strong willed. Offer yourself to me, an everlasting
holocaust with your heart as the altar of sacrifice, for
the glory of my name. Put your body and your soul
trustfully in my care. This is the way to become fit
to begin to offer sacrifice to God, to receive with
wholesomeness the sacrament of my body.

No offering is fitter, nothing serves better to wash
away sins than the pure total offering of yourself along
with the offering of Christ's body in the Mass and in
communion. If a man does his best to repent, whenever
he comes to me for pardon and for grace, *as I live – it
is the Lord Yahweh who speaks – I take pleasure, not
in the death of a wicked man, but in the turning back
of a wicked man who changes his ways to win life* (Ez

33: 11), I will remember his sins no longer. I will forgive them all.

CHAPTER EIGHT

Christ's Offering on the Cross

The Beloved Says: I offered myself willingly to God the Father for your sins. My arms were stretched on the cross. My body was naked. There was nothing in me that was not totally transformed into a sacrifice begging God's forgiveness. In the same way, with all the might and affection you can find within yourself, you too should make a pure, holy, willing offering of yourself in daily Mass. I can ask nothing more of you except that you strive to be completely under me. I have no regard for anything you give beyond yourself. I do not want your gifts, just you.

To own everything, but not me, could not satisfy you. In the same way, whatever you offer cannot please me unless you offer yourself too. Offer yourself to me. Give yourself completely to God. An offering such as this will be acceptable. I offered myself completely to the Father for you. I gave my whole body and blood as food so that I should be completely yours and you should be mine. If you want to stand on your own, unwilling to submit to my will, your sacrifice is incomplete and there is no real union between us. If you wish to receive freedom and grace, a free offering of yourself into God's hands must come before everything you do. It is for this reason that so few are really free and enlightened. For they do not know how to deny themselves fully.

My decision is firm: *none of you can be my disciple unless he gives up all his possessions* (Lk 14: 33). If I choose you to be my disciple, offer me yourself and all your love.

CHAPTER NINE

Offer God Everything

The Disciple Says: Lord, everything in heaven and on earth is yours. I want to make a generous offering of myself to you. I want to be yours always. Lord, my intention is pure. I offer myself to you. I want to be your servant for ever, to worship you and to become for you a sacrifice of everlasting praise. Accept me along with the offering of your precious body. I offer it daily to you in the presence of the angels. For, though they are not seen, yet they are there. May this offering bring about the salvation of myself and of all people.

On this altar, Lord, I offer you all the sins and offenses I have committed before you and your holy angels from the time I was first able to sin up till now. May the fire of your love burn them and consume them. Clean my conscience of every fault. Restore to me the grace I lost by sinning. Forgive me everything fully and embrace me in a merciful kiss of peace.

What can I do about my sins? I can only confess them, grieve for them and never stop begging your forgiveness. Listen to me with kindness, my God, I beg you, when I stand before you. All my sins disgust me. I do not wish to do them ever again. I am sorry for them. I will weep over them as long as I live. I am ready to do penance and to do what I can to make amends. Release me, God, release me from my sins and preserve the holiness of your name. Save this soul of mine that your precious blood has redeemed. I leave myself in your mercy. I put myself in your hands.

Do to me not what my wickedness and sinfulness deserve, but what your goodness desires.

I offer you whatever good I own, small and faulty as it is. Repair it and make it holy. You can make it pleasant and acceptable. You can turn it into something better. Though I am a useless, lazy fellow, you can take the good I do and bring it to a happy, worthwhile conclusion.

I bring you also all the good intentions of devoted people, the needs of my parents, of friends, of brothers, of sisters, of all I love and of all that have done me and others good. I bring you the needs of all those who have asked for my prayers and Masses for themselves and for their relatives, both living and dead. I make this offering that all may come to know the benefit of your grace, the blessing of your comfort, protection from danger and remission of punishment. May they be saved from every evil and praise you with joy and gratitude.

I bring you my prayers and my sacrifices especially for those who have wronged me, for those who have made me sad and have slandered me, for those who have harmed and annoyed me. I offer them also for all those who were made sad sometimes, were upset, annoyed or scandalised by what I said or did, wittingly or unwittingly. Forgive us all our sins and the wrongs we do to one another. Free our hearts, Lord, from all suspicion, anger, wrath, contention, from whatever can wound charity and lessen brotherly love. Have mercy, Lord, have mercy on those who beg your mercy. Grant your grace to those who need it. Make us all live in such a way that we may enjoy the benefits of your grace and reach everlasting life. Amen.

CHAPTER TEN

Do Not Easily Omit Communion

The Beloved Says: You must return frequently to the source of divine grace and mercy, the fount of purity and goodness. In this way you may be cured of your lusts and your vices. You will be made strong in the face of all the devil's temptations and tricks. The enemy appreciates how greatly holy communion restores the spirit. In so far as he can, in every way, when opportunity arises, he tries to pull faithful and devout persons away from it.

Some people suffer Satan's worst attacks when they set themselves to prepare for holy communion. This wicked spirit (as it is written in Job) comes among the sons of God to upset them with the malice he knows how to employ. He makes them very timid and confused. He weakens their devotion. He tries by his attacks to take away their faith. His aim is to make them give up the idea of going to communion or make them lukewarm in their approach to it. You must not bother about his tricks or the dirty horrid thoughts he suggests. Throw all these thoughts back at his head. Condemn this wretched person and laugh at him. Do not omit holy communion because of his attacks or the trouble he stirs up.

Common hindrances are too great concern about being full of devotion and worry about going to confession. Take the advice of people who are wise. Get rid of worry and scruple. They block God's grace and destroy that devotion which is of the mind. Do not put off communion because you are vexed or troubled. Be quick to go to confession. Be glad to forgive others all the wrongs they do you. Humbly beg pardon of anyone you have offended and God will be pleased to forgive you.

What good do you do yourself when you delay confession or postpone communion? Purge yourself immediately. Spit out the poison quickly. Be quick to use the remedy. You will feel better if you do not put it off too long. If today brings one reason to omit communion, tomorrow perhaps will bring a greater reason for doing so. The longer you stay away from communion, the more unfit you will be. Cut out this weariness and sloth as quick as you can. To be constantly worried and upset or to allow daily obstacles to keep you from the divine mysteries does you no good. To stay away from communion for a long time actually harms you. Its common result is great indifference. The pity is that some lukewarm, careless people are glad to delay confession and postpone holy communion in order to be free of the obligation to keep a firmer grip on themselves.

What little charity, what poor devotion is possessed by those who easily postpone holy communion! That man is happy and acceptable to God, who keeps his conscience clean and lives in such a way that he is ready to go to communion even daily. How much good he would gain from this, if he were allowed to do so and could manage to do it without being singled out! When a man abstains from humility or because of some legitimate impediment, he is to be praised. But whenever a man is full of sloth he should do what he can to rouse himself. The Lord who has special consideration for his good intentions will aid him in his desires.

If a man like that is legitimately excluded from communion, he should make an act of the will and fix his good intentions on communion. In this way he will not lose the benefit of the sacrament. Any devout person can practise spiritual communion every day and all day. It is a wholesome thing to do. It is not forbidden. Yet, at set times and on fixed days, he should receive the body of his redeemer sacramentally with reverent devotion. In this he should seek to praise and honour God rather than seek his own comfort. Every time a man recalls the mystery of Christ's incarnation and remembers with devotion the sufferings of Christ he is set on fire with love, he communicates mystically and enjoys unseen refreshment.

A man who makes ready to communicate only at the time of great festivals or when custom demands it is often unprepared. That man is happy who offers himself as a sacrifice to the Lord whenever he celebrates Mass or goes to communion. Do not celebrate Mass too slowly or too quickly. Follow the normal custom of those among whom you live. You should not annoy others or be a bother to them. Follow

whatever norm the superiors have laid down. You are
to serve the convenience of others, not your own
devotion or inclination.

CHAPTER ELEVEN

The Soul Needs Christ and Holy Writ

The Disciple Says: Most delightful Lord Jesus, the
devout soul has great delight indeed when she eats at
your table. There the food she is given to eat is none
other than you, her only love, more desirable than
anything that can be desired. I would be delighted
indeed if I could weep tears of deep affection in your
presence, if, like Magdalen, I could wash your feet
with my tears. Where can I find such devotion? Where
can I discover this bubbling flood of holy tears? In the
presence of you and of your holy angels my heart
should certainly be aflame. It would weep for joy. For
I possess you really present in this sacrament, though
you hide yourself under another guise.

If you showed yourself in all your own divine
splendour, my eyes could not look on you. The whole
world has not the strength to stand in the bright light
of your majestic glory. You hide yourself in the sacrament out of consideration for my weakness. The one
whom I possess and adore is the same as the angels
adore in heaven. For the time being, I adore by the
light of faith. They adore what they see uncovered.
I should be satisfied with the light of faith. I should
go where it leads until the day of everlasting splendour
dawns and the shades that appearances provide are let

down. *But once perfection comes* (1 Cor 13: 10) the sacraments will be used no more. Those who are blessed with heavenly glory need no sacramental medicine. They rejoice for ever with God. They gaze on his glory set out before their eyes. They are lifted into the sheer brightness of the godhead's depth and taste the word of God made flesh, as he was in the beginning and shall always be.

When my mind is on these wonders, even spiritual comforts become wearisome to me. As long as I do not see my Lord's uncovered glory I put no value on what is seen or heard on earth. You are my witness, God. Nothing can console me. Nothing can bring me peace. Only you, my God, whom I desire to contemplate for ever. But while death has hold on me this is not possible. I must be very patient. I must submit myself and all I desire to you. Your saints indeed, Lord, already rejoice with you in glory. But, while they lived, they were faithful and very patient as they awaited the coming of your glory. What they believed I believe. The hope they had is also mine. Where they have arrived I trust your grace to help me reach. Faith guides my steps. The saints' example gives me strength. Holy books shall be my comforts and my guides in life. Along with all these your holy body will be my special remedy and recourse.

I feel that two things in life are supremely necessary. Without them this unhappy life would be unbearable. While I am imprisoned in this body, I confess to the need of two things: food and light. I am weak. So you have given me your holy body as food for mind and body. You have given me *your word* as *a lamp for my feet* (Ps 119: 105). I could not live at all without these

two things. The word of God is the light of my soul.
Your sacrament is the bread of life. These can be called
the two tables set side by side in the church's treasure
house. One table is the holy altar, holding the holy
bread that is Christ's precious body. The other is God's
law, holding the holy doctrine. It teaches true faith
that pierces right beyond the veil that leads to the
holy of holies. We thank you, Lord Jesus, gleam of
light that does not fail. You have given us the table
of holy doctrine through your servants, the prophets,
the apostles and other holy teachers.

We thank you, man's creator and redeemer. To
show your love for all the world, you have prepared
a great supper. The food you have offered us is no
symbolic lamb, but your own body and blood. Your
banquet brings joy to all faithful men, makes them
drunk with the cup that saves us and contains the
delights of paradise. With even greater enjoyment the
holy angels join us in the feast.

What a great honour is the task of the priest! He
may use the sacred words to consecrate the Lord of
Majesty, bless him with his lips, hold him in his
hands, take him in his own mouth and give him to
others. How clean must be those hands! How pure
that mouth! How stainless should the priest's heart
be! The source of purity comes to him so often!
Nothing but what is holy, nothing but what is noble
and fitting should come out of the mouth of the priest.
For he receives Christ's sacrament so often. Those
eyes, so accustomed to look on Christ's body, should
be sound and modest. Those hands, accustomed to
holding the creator of heaven and earth, should be
clean, raised heavenwards. The Law speaks specially

of priests: *Be holy, for I, Yahweh, your God, am holy* (Lev 19: 2).

O Almighty God, may your grace help us who have received the office of the priesthood so that we may serve you fittingly, devotedly, with all modesty and cleanness of conscience. If we cannot live as guiltlessly as we ought, make us weep over the wrongs we have done. Give us a humble spirit. Grant a firmness to our good intention of serving you with greater fervour for the rest of our lives.

CHAPTER TWELVE

Prepare for Christ Diligently

The Beloved Says: I am the one who loves purity and gives all holiness. I seek a pure heart where I might rest. Make ready for me *a large supper room furnished with couches* (Mk 14: 15). There I will eat the passover with you and my disciples. You want me to come and stay with you? Then cast out the old leaven. Make your heart a clean house. Shut out the world and all the noisiness of vice. Sit like *a lone bird on the rooftop* (Ps 102: 8). Think of the wrongs you have done, your soul full of bitterness. Every lover prepares the best and prettiest place for the one he loves. By entertaining his beloved in this way he makes his affection known.

Be aware that your own efforts cannot prepare you sufficiently for this, even if you spent a year at it and had nothing else in mind. My kindness and grace alone are what allows you to come to my table. You are like a beggar invited to come and share a rich man's meal. Nothing that you own can reward him. You must be meek and simply thankful. Do what you can. What you do do diligently, not because it is the done thing or because you have to. Receive the body of your beloved lord and God with fear, reverence and love, when he honours you with a visit. I have given the call. I have given the command. I will supply what you lack. Come and take me.

If I give you devotion, be thankful. Although you are not worthy, I have had mercy on you. If you have no devotion and feel very arid, keep praying, cry and keep knocking. Do not stop until you earn a crumb or drop of saving grace. You need me. I do not need you. You do not make me holy; it is I who make you holy and bring you improvement. You come to me to be one with me and share my holiness so that you may gain fresh grace and burn with desire for improvement. Do not ignore this grace. Be energetic in preparing your heart to receive your beloved.

You must make yourself ready to be devout before communion. You must keep it up after you have received the sacrament. A guard afterwards is no less necessary than was devout preparation beforehand. This after care of good is the very best preparation for receiving further grace. A man becomes less well disposed when he rushes off immediately to enjoy outward comforts. Beware of chatter. Keep yourself to yourself. Then you may enjoy your God. For you own him and the world cannot take him away from you. You must give yourself completely to me so that you live no longer for your own sake, but only for me.

CHAPTER THIRTEEN

Desire for Union with Christ

The Disciple Says: Who will let me meet you alone, Lord, to open my heart to you and have with you the pleasure that my soul seeks *without people thinking ill of me* (Song 8: 1)? Let no created thing influence me or be influenced by me. Let you and me speak to each other alone as is the way of the lover to his loved one or a friend to a friend. I pray for this. I want it. Let me be wholly one with you. Let me pull my heart away from every created thing. Through frequent communion and celebration of holy Mass let me learn a taste for the things that last in heaven. O Lord God! When shall I be wholly one with you, steeped in you, completely forgetful of self? You are in me and I in you. Let us both go on being one.

You are indeed *my Beloved . . . to be known among ten thousand* (Song 5: 10), *the favourite of my soul* (Mt 12: 18), whose company I wish to enjoy every day of my life. You bring me peace, peace that is perfect and rest that is real. Without you there is only toil, sorrow and boundless unhappiness. You are indeed a hidden God. The wicked ignore your advice. Your word comes to the meek and the simple hearted. How gentle is your spirit, Lord! To show your sweetness to your children, you refresh them with that sweetest bread from heaven. *And indeed, what great nation is there that has its gods as near as Yahweh our God is to us* (Deut 4: 7)? You are near to those who believe in you. You give yourself as food that is to be enjoyed as daily comfort and lifts the heart to heaven.

What people is so renowned as the christian people?
What created thing under the sky is so loved as that
devoted soul whom God enters to feed her with his
glorious flesh? O indescribable grace! O admirable
kindness! O immense love, poured out on man alone!
What can I give back to God in return for this grace,
this excellent love? The gift by which I can please
him best is the complete surrender of my heart to
become closely one with God. When my soul is united
with God, all that is in me will heave with joy. God
will say to me: I want to be with you if you want to
be with me. And I will reply: Please stay with me,
Lord. I want to be glad with you. All I desire is a heart
that is one with you.

CHAPTER FOURTEEN

Ardent Desire for the Body of Christ

The Disciple Says: Yahweh, how great is your goodness
reserved for those who fear you (Ps 31: 19). I am often
embarrassed and ashamed when I think of some
devoted people who come to your sacrament, Lord,
with such great devotion and fervour. For I am so
lukewarm and cold when I approach your altar, the
table of your holy communion. I remain dry, without
any fervour in my heart. Your presence, Lord, does
not set me on fire. I am not as strongly attracted, not
as full of affection as were many devoted people. Their
desire for communion and their heartfelt love was
such that they could not hold back their tears. They
sighed in the depths of their hearts and bodies for you,

God, the source of life. They could control and satisfy their hunger only by receiving your body with joyful spiritual eagerness.

O the sheer fire of their faith! An argument suggesting your sacred presence in them! They are the ones who recognise the Lord *in the breaking of bread* (Lk 24: 35), whose hearts burned within them when Jesus walked along with them. Such feeling and devotion, such love and fervour are often far from me. Good Jesus, be gracious to me. Be sweet and kind. Let poor me who entreats you feel sometimes at least a little heartfelt, loving affection when he receives your holy communion. Make my faith strong. Give me hope of progress. Fire me at least once with perfect charity. Let me taste the heavenly manna and never falter.

Your mercy is able to grant me the grace I desire. Whenever it pleases you, your bounty can come to me and pay me a gentle visit. I may not burn with a desire equal to that of the specially devoted. Yet, by your grace, I long to be on fire with that desire. I pray and seek to become one of the host of your specially ardent lovers. I would like to be listed in their holy company-

CHAPTER FIFTEEN

Devotion - Humility - Self-Denial

The Beloved Says: You should always seek the grace of devotion. Ask for it with sincerity. Wait for it with patient trust. Accept it with thanks. Keep it with humility. Strive to work with it. Put yourself in the hands of God in matters concerning when and how he will visit you when he comes. You must be specially humble when you feel little or no devotion. Do not become too upset or give yourself up to uncontrolled grief. God gives always in a short instant what he has denied you for a long time. He grants sometimes at the end of prayer what he took away at the beginning.

If grace was always given quickly or could always be had for the asking, weak man could not stand it. For this reason, the grace of devotion is to be awaited with good hope and humble patience. When it is not given, or even quietly taken away, blame yourself and your sins. It takes a small thing sometimes to block and conceal grace. Perhaps we should not call it a little thing, but something big, which blocks so much good. When you have got rid of this big or little thing you will have what you asked.

As soon as you have surrendered your whole heart to God, asking neither for one thing nor for another that you fancy or desire and placing yourself totally in God's hands, you will find peace and recollection. There is nothing serves you better or gives you pleasure so great as what is pleasing to God's will. Whoever lifts his mind up to God with sincerity of heart and empties himself of all undisciplined love or dislike of created things will be very fit to receive grace and worthy of the gift of devotion. God fills with his blessing the vessel he finds empty. Grace will come more quickly to the one who renounces earthly things more perfectly and dies to himself more thoroughly. Its entry will be larger and it will raise his heart higher.

Then he will see and become rich. He will wonder. His heart will expand. For God's hand is with him. He has placed himself in God's hands for ever. Such will be the blessing gained by a man who seeks God with all his heart, *whose soul does not pay homage to worthless things* (Ps 24: 4). By receiving holy communion such a man earns the great grace of union with God. For he does not seek his own comfort and devotion, but only such comfort and devotion as gives glory and honour to God.

CHAPTER SIXTEEN

Let Christ Know Your Needs

The Disciple Says: Most sweet and loving Lord, I wish to receive you. You know that I suffer from weakness and I am in need. You know the size of the ills and evils to which I am subject, how often I am weary, tempted, disturbed and defiled. I come to you for medicine. I beg you to console and support me. I speak to you who know all and see clearly all that is inside me. You alone can help me and console me fully. You know how poor I am in virtue and the good things I lack especially.

I stand before you, naked and poor, asking your grace and begging your mercy. Hungry, I beg you to feed me. Set my soul alight with the fire of your love. Light up my blindness with the splendour of your presence. Make all earthly things bitter to me. Make me patient with weariness and opposition. Make me condemn and ignore all things created and all that is base. Lift my heart up to you in heaven. Do not let me stray about on earth, May you alone be my everlasting delight. You alone are my food and my drink, my love and my gladness, my delight and all the good I have.

Would that your presence would set me totally aflame, burn me up and change me into you. Make me one with you in spirit by the grace of inward union, melting me with burning love. Do not let me leave you, hungry and parched. In your mercy, do to me the wonderful things you often did to your saints. It would be no marvel if I were set aflame by you and crumbled away. Are you not the fire that always burns and is never quenched? Are you not the love that cleans the heart and lights up the mind?

CHAPTER SEVENTEEN

Burning Desire for Christ

The Disciple Says: I desire to receive you, Lord, with the greatest devotion and burning love just as many saints and committed persons desired to receive you in communion. Their great holiness of life pleased you very much. Their devotion to you was very ardent. O my God, love that lasts for ever, all the good I have, happiness that is unending! I have the most strong desire to receive you with the greatest reverence any saint ever had or could have felt.

I may be unfit to have all these feelings of devotion. Yet I offer all the affection of my heart as if I were alone in having such pleasant burning desires. I present

and offer to you all that the pious mind can think of
and desire. I offer it with the greatest adoration and
inward fervour. I want to keep nothing for myself.
Willingly and gladly I sacrifice myself and all I have.
Lord, my God, my creator, my redeemer, I want to
welcome you today with the same affection, reverence,
praise, glory, thankfulness, dignity, love, faith, hope,
the same purity as your most holy mother welcomed
and desired you with. When she, the glorious Virgin
Mary, received from the angel the good news of the
incarnation, she replied with meek devotion: *I am the
handmaid of the Lord . . . Let what you have said be
done to me* (Lk 1: 38).

Your blessed forerunner, John the Baptist, most
excellent of the saints, was filled with joy of the spirit
in your presence. He jumped for joy while still
enclosed in his mother's womb. Later, when he saw
Jesus walking among men, he humbled himself and
declared with devout affection: *The bridegroom's
friend, when he stands there and listens, is glad when
he hears the bridegroom's voice* (Jn 3: 29). I too want
to be on fire with the same great and holy desires, to
offer myself to you with all my heart. Therefore I
display and offer you the joys that are in the hearts of
all devoted people, their ardent love, their mental·
raptures, their supernatural enlightenment, their
heavenly visions with all the virtues and praises that
have been celebrated and are to be celebrated by
creatures in heaven and on earth. I offer them for
myself and for all who have been commended to my
prayers. May you be praised worthily and glorified for
ever by everyone.

My Lord and God, accept my vows, the desires I

have for the unbounded praises and tremendous blessings that are your right. For you are great beyond
measure and description. I have a great desire to give
you these every day, every moment of time. With
loving prayers I invite and exhort all the faithful and
every heavenly spirit to join me in thanks and praise.

Let all nations, tribes and tongues praise you. Let
them glorify your sweet and holy name with greatest
joy and burning devotion. May all who celebrate the
most high sacrament with reverent devotion and all
who communicate in full faith earn the reward of
finding your grace and mercy. May they pray for me
also. For I am a sinner. When they receive the joy
they yearned for, when they have enjoyed union with
you, when they leave the sacred heavenly table, filled
with comfort, please let them remember me, a sinner.

CHAPTER EIGHTEEN

Submission to Christ in Faith

The Beloved Says: Curious futile examination of this
most profound sacrament is something you must avoid.
In this way you will not be sunk in the depths of
doubt.

Search too high and the depths will dazzle thee (Prov
25: 27). God can do more things than man can understand. A man may search into the truth with meekness
and devotion; but he should be ready to learn and seek
to follow the sound opinions of the fathers.

Happy is that simplicity which rejects tortuous
means of inquiry and walks firmly in the straight

steps of God's commandments. Many have sought to study too profoundly. In this way they lost devotion. Faith and sincerity of life are what is required of you, not intellectual greatness, and not deep study of God's mysteries. If you can neither grasp nor understand what is beneath you, how can you comprehend what is above you? Place yourself under God. Make your understanding subject to faith. You will be given such light of knowledge as will be suitable and necessary for you.

Some men have serious temptations concerning faith and this sacrament. They are not to be blamed. Better blame the enemy. Do not worry. Do not fight your own thoughts. Do not answer the doubts the devil has sent you. Trust God's words. Believe his saints and prophets. Then the wicked enemy will run away from you. It is sometimes helpful for the servant of God to suffer in this way. For the devil does not tempt and pester infidels and sinners. He is sure he owns them. It is the faithful and devout whom he tempts and worries in many ways.

Proceed then with simple undoubting faith. Come to the sacrament with prayerful reverence. Place whatever you cannot understand in God's safe care. God will not deceive you. The man who trusts too much in himself is the one who is deceived. God walks with the simple. He makes children understand. He reveals his meaning to minds that are pure. He hides his grace from those who are proud and curious. Human reason is weak. It can be deceived. But real faith cannot be deceived.

Reason and natural inquiry should always follow faith. They should not come before faith or challenge it. In this matter, faith and love are most important. The ways they work in the most holy and excellent sacrament are obscure. The eternal God has great and unlimited power. The great things he does in heaven and on earth are not measurable. His wonders are not to be examined. If human reason could grasp easily the works of God, then these works could not be wonders. We could not say they are indescribable.